D1444198

The United States

ONE DOLLA

DEPRESSA RESURGIT

Printed by HALL and SELLERS

THE UNITED STATES ensure the
ment of the within BILL, and will d
Bills of Exchange for the Interest annuall
demanded, according to a Resolution of C
GRESS, of the 18th of March, 1780.

Jon Arnol

UNITED STATES

# Hamilton

## FOUNDING FATHER

# Hamilton

## FOUNDING FATHER

*MARIE RAPHAEL*
*RAY RAPHAEL*

## FALL RIVER PRESS

New York

## FALL RIVER PRESS

New York

An Imprint of Sterling Publishing Co., Inc.
1166 Avenue of the Americas
New York, NY 10036

FALL RIVER PRESS and the distinctive Fall River Press logo are
registered trademarks of Barnes & Noble Booksellers, Inc.

© 2017 Marie Raphael, Ray Raphael

All rights reserved. No part of this publication may be reproduced,
stored in a retrieval system, or transmitted in any form or by any means
(including electronic, mechanical, photocopying, recording, or otherwise)
without prior written permission from the publisher.

ISBN 978-1-4351-6641-7

Distributed in the United Kingdom by GMC Distribution Services
Castle Place, 166 High Street, Lewes, East Sussex, England BN7 1XU
Distributed in Australia by NewSouth Books
45 Beach Street, Coogee, NSW 2034, Australia

For information about custom editions, special sales, and premium and
corporate purchases, please contact Sterling Special Sales at 800-805-5489
or specialsales@sterlingpublishing.com.

Manufactured in China

2  4  6  8  10  9  7  5  3  1

sterlingpublishing.com

Book design by Kevin Ullrich

# Contents

# Prologue

WHO WERE THE FOUNDING FATHERS? IN REALITY, THOUSANDS OF patriots helped build the nation, but Americans focus on only a handful of venerated candidates. Although Alexander Hamilton made it on to that short list, he doesn't have much in common with his fellow Founding Fathers.

At the head of the line is George Washington, our first president. For that and much else he has garnered the title Father of Our Country. The next president was John Adams, followed by Thomas Jefferson and James Madison. The Massachusetts-born Adams could point to an impeccable American lineage—a great-great-grandfather had arrived on the Mayflower. The others, all Virginians, were born into landed gentry and derived their wealth from plantations worked by slaves.

Another celebrated founder, Benjamin Franklin, did not have much in the way of lineage or wealth, but he seems more American than any other. The prototypical self-made man, he was the celebrated inventor-scientist and the wit who gave his countrymen *Poor Richard's Almanac*. Franklin was also a canny diplomat. In France, when seeking aid for the American Revolution, he donned a coonskin hat, a calculated act that charmed dukes and duchesses.

Alexander Hamilton was neither a charmer nor a celebrity. He was not landed or native-born, and, technically, at birth he was illegitimate. He never became president. Even so, Hamilton stands alongside the others on the national stage. As the saying goes, this founder seemed to "come out of nowhere," but Hamilton did have a home—West Indian islands set in the Caribbean Sea.

The islands offered instruction to an inquisitive boy who noted all that transpired in the world around him. Enslaved Africans worked the plantations and vastly outnumbered whites, whose brutal laws kept them in place. The economy depended on a preeminent commodity, sugar, which was vulnerable to whatever might befall the crop or rock the market. European nations extracted island wealth, their needs trumping those of the locals. A strict, hierarchical governance resisted remedies of any kind. By the time Hamilton left the islands as a teen, he could imagine a better way of doing things.

On the mainland of North America, the newly arrived immigrant found colonists who defied British imperial rule. Hamilton embraced their cause and wrote pamphlets to promote it. When actual fighting broke out, he joined the army. War gave him his chance. He rose quickly through the ranks to become an aide-de-camp to Commander-in-Chief George Washington. At Washington's side over the space of four years, Hamilton saw up close the snags and stumbling blocks of a struggling, infant nation. Congressional lethargy and neglect hampered the war effort. The commissary's ineptitude meant that soldiers lacked blankets or shoes or food or even bullets. In the Caribbean, there had been too much order. In the American colonies, there was too little.

After the war, thirteen states vied for power, yanking this way and that on the reins of government. Hamilton and others worried that if state interests trumped federal ones, the country might not survive. They called for a convention and devised a system—a new Constitution—that put national interests first. When arguing for the ratification of these new rules, Hamilton maintained that government would not take liberty away but protect it. "The vigor of government is essential to the security of liberty," he wrote.

For Hamilton, a paper plan was only the beginning. To establish a strong financial footing, America had to raise money and retire its war debts. As the first Secretary of the Treasury, he called for the levying of taxes—his poll numbers dropped. He pushed for a national bank—also a contentious affair.

In the early years of the young republic, Hamilton more than anyone set the political agenda. He made progress and he made enemies, but in the end, the credit of the United States was solid. Once an outsider, Hamilton became the quintessential insider—the man who made government work even if he had to connive and finagle and defeat disgruntled, rebellious taxpayers to do it.

Whenever Hamilton saw something that was broken—whether a dysfunctional system of government or the financial insolvency of the nation—he tried to fix it. He helped to found the New York Manumission Society and detailed procedures for owners who wished to free their slaves. Since smuggling cost the nation revenues, he instituted a Customs Service to put an end to it. A repairman at heart, he was in addition the engineer who pored over the infinitesimal specifications of his many ventures. Policing the waters required lighthouses, so he designed them. Lighthouses required whale oil to beam light onto black waters, and he had a particular type in mind. Nothing daunted him and nothing fell below his notice.

Hamilton was a complex and fully human character. For all of his political victories, there were also dire lapses of judgment. After years of marital ardor and fidelity, he indulged in reckless adultery. In public he was the hard moneyman, but he devotedly nursed his children when they were sick. He lashed out at civic enemies, but he sat beside his daughter Angelica to play duets. When she suffered a mental collapse, he did all he could to find parakeets to give her because she was enamored of birds. As his final act, the nation's forward-looking pragmatist died for honor's sake, an ill-thought-out conclusion. His wife and children bore the consequences.

This founding father was a polarizing figure. Like his contemporaries, historians have taken sides. Was he a friend of liberty or its enemy? How do we know? The best evidence lies in primary source records from Hamilton's own time. After his death, layer upon layer of storytelling was added. When we peel back those layers, we close in on the truth.

Reader, meet Alexander Hamilton.

# 1755–1773

# The Sugar Islands

ALEXANDER HAMILTON'S FAMILY MADE A HOME ON NEVIS AND eventually ST. Croix, lush West Indian islands set in a blue sea and rimmed by white coral beaches. For a privileged class, these islands were a paradise. But it was a hard-scrabble paradise for those who tried to maintain a footing on financially slippery ground, as Hamilton's parents did. The destitute came, serving as indentured servants if need be, customarily trading seven years of their life for passage. Adventurers and petty criminals also arrived, ready for anything, whether illicit or licit. Buccaneers and pirates made an appearance, though demoted and no longer serving as a marauding force for one European power or another. And then there were those carried to the Caribbean from Africa on slave ships. They swiftly descended into hell.

# "Bastard Brat of a Scottish Peddler"

Columbus originally sighted the egg-shaped island of Nevis in 1493 and claimed it for Spain, disregarding, as all European powers did, the natural title of the indigenous inhabitants. By the time Alexander Hamilton made his appearance, the island was under British control and had been for more than a century. Even though it measured only eight miles long and six miles across at its widest, Nevis was an imperial treasure trove. Sugarcane grew tall in its fields. Ships sailed from its harbor carrying the processed sequel, a commodity desired the world over and dubbed "white gold." In 1759 William Pitt the Elder, Britain's prime minister, estimated that the empire derived four times as much income from the West Indies as from other global holdings.[1] It is no wonder that violent skirmishes were a fact of life in the Caribbean over the centuries, with islands changing hands and serving as pawns in a global contest for riches.

Rachel Fawcett gave birth to Alexander Hamilton on Nevis in 1755, or so Alexander's uncle testified in probate court following her death. (Although Hamilton later claimed a birthdate of 1757, the earlier one is credible and widely accepted.) Another son watched his mother nurse the mottled newborn. This was two-year-old James, who was named after his father, James Hamilton. Alexander and James would spend their childhood days together, but Rachel's first-born, Peter, was entirely absent from this family unit. He was nine years Alexander's senior and bore the surname Lavien. His father, Johann Michael Lavien, was still, by law, Rachel's husband and so, when decades later John Adams called Alexander Hamilton the "bastard brat of a Scottish Peddler," he was technically correct. The explanation is longer and more forgiving.[2]

In 1745, when Rachel was only sixteen, she inherited her father's small sugar estate on Nevis along with his other holdings. Soon after,

The Alexander Hamilton Museum in Nevis is built on the foundation of the house (destroyed by an earthquake in 1840) where Hamilton was born

accompanied by her mother, Mary, the bright, young heiress travelled to the island of St. Croix, one day's sail to the west. It was a likely destination for two women in suddenly altered circumstances since Rachel's sister, Ann, already lived there on a sugar plantation with her husband, James Lytton. Rachel was attractive and her inheritance—what Alexander Hamilton later dubbed "a *snug* fortune"—undoubtedly added to her attractions. This is when Johann Michael Lavien entered the story. He was a dashing man, at least a decade older than Rachel. His finances were seemingly secure, although in reality he was seriously in debt to the Danish West India Company.[3] In Alexander's telling many years later, Lavien was nothing more than "a fortune-hunter" who was "bedizzened with gold," but an unsuspecting Mary Fawcett took him at face value. She encouraged her daughter to accept his advances. Rachel was swayed and married him, and a year later Peter was born—Rachel's eldest son, half-brother to two later sons James and Alexander.[4]

Five years later the marriage was in shambles and Rachel left her husband. Lavien accused her of adultery. St. Croix at the time was owned by Denmark, and under Danish law, an adulteress who had deserted her husband could be jailed for the offense. Upon Lavien's insistence, Rachel was confined to a cramped cell in Christiansted's fort for several months, sustained only by scant rations. Lavien expected his wife to be more compliant after her punishment, but he underestimated her resolve. Upon her release Rachel immediately bolted to the British-controlled island of St. Kitts, out of Lavien's reach. It was separated by only a two-mile-wide channel from Nevis, the island of her childhood, where she had known safety. She left not only a husband but her young son, Peter.

In 1759, when seeking a divorce, Johann Lavien called his wife "shameless, coarse, and ungodly" and said she had "completely forgotten her duty and let husband and child alone and instead given herself up to whoring with everyone." His estate, he declared, must never be given to her "whore children."[5] It's impossible to document Rachel's guilt or innocence, but the wording of the accusations—along with her early, aberrant jailing—points to Lavien's abusive nature. In turn, Rachel's flight, while evidence of her real fear, also suggests that she was not as biddable as others of her age and sex might be. Barely out of her teens, she refused to succumb to marital cruelty or to court admonishments and had a sense of her own natural rights.

In St. Kitts Rachel met James Hamilton, the "Scottish Peddler" whom John Adams referenced in his mocking assessment of Alexander Hamilton. In truth, James had a prestigious lineage Adams did not mention. His maternal grandfather was a baronet and member, first of the Scottish Parliament, and then, after the 1807 Act of Union, the British Parliament.

James's father, Alexander's namesake, was the fourteenth Laird of the Grange in the Ayrshire parish of Stevenston. In 1685 the family acquired nearby Kerelaw Castle, which dated back to the fifteenth century.[6] James grew up in this castle, which the family affectionately called "The Grange"—connoting a large country house for a secure, landed family.

Following the laws of primogeniture, James's oldest brother, John, eventually inherited the castle, the lands, the monies, and the title. Nonetheless, John Hamilton assisted all of his siblings and paid for James's four-year apprenticeship in linen manufacturing. As soon as that ended, James quit the business and quit Scotland as well. His sights set higher; he took himself off to the West Indies, as bold young men were then doing. He aspired to commercial trading, a lucrative business. But traders succeeded best if they had ample capital, which secured them during a downswing and permitted investment during an upswing. Unfortunately, James lacked both money and a head for high finance. His fortunes often shifting, he supported himself by any means necessary. John Hamilton apparently kept an eye on his wayward sibling. At times he paid off James's creditors or fostered a connection between James and his own island associates.

For years Rachel and James could not marry because Johann Lavien would not countenance a divorce. When Lavien finally obtained a divorce so *he* could marry again, he ensured the terms stipulated that *she* could not. A common-law marriage was not uncommon, however, and Rachel and James's union seems to have lasted fifteen years. Its durability suggests an actual bond, especially since Rachel had it in her to quit a marriage if she had to and she did not quit this one.

FOLLOWING: Map of St. Kitts (also sometimes referred to as St. Christophers), with inset of Nevis, 1775

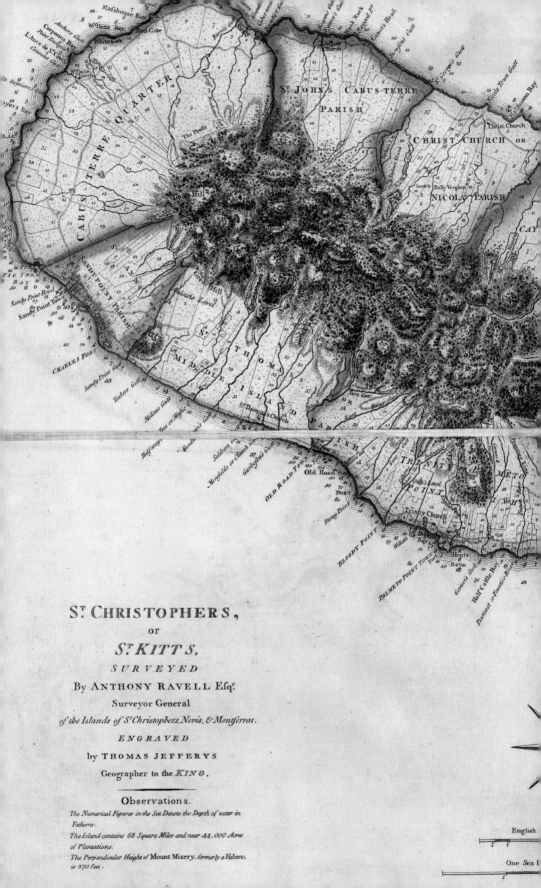

# ST. CHRISTOPHERS,
### or
## ST. KITTS,
#### SURVEYED
#### By ANTHONY RAVELL Esq.
Surveyor General
*of the Islands of St. Christophers, Nevis, & Montserrat.*

#### ENGRAVED
#### by THOMAS JEFFERYS
Geographer to the *KING*.

### Observations.

*The Numerical Figures in the Sea Denote the Depth of water in Fathoms.*

*The Island contains 68 Square Miles and near 44,000 Acres of Plantations.*

*The Perpendicular Height of Mount Misery, formerly a Volcano, is 3711 Feet.*

English

One Sea l

# An Island Heritage

Before long James and Rachel crossed the strait that divided St. Kitts from Nevis, in all probability taking up residence in a building on the Charlestown waterfront that Rachel's father had bequeathed her. It was on Nevis that sons James and Alexander passed their early boyhood years. The household ran along in its skitter-scatter way. Alexander's parents swatted at everyday debts and worries, but there was no getting rid of them. Like buzzing flies, they repeatedly circled back. In the meantime Hamilton's father jabbered on at times about his noble lineage, the Scottish peaks where sheep ran, the rugged Ayrshire coast, and Kerelaw Castle, with its solid walls and grand halls. From time to time his mother reflected on her more affluent and honorable childhood. The disparity in fortune must have struck Hamilton and sparked ambition—if he were somehow due more, how could he get it? How could he reverse this downward spiral? How could he rise?

The boy was not formally schooled but tutored. Preternaturally observant and eager, he would have squeezed all the knowledge he could from his sessions with an instructor, most likely one of the elderly Jewish women who assumed this role on Nevis. He developed a taste for orderly columns of figures. He deciphered words and raced through text and was, before long, ready to take on the books in his family's small library, the thirty-four volumes he treasured.

Outside the modest home quarters, Hamilton ran along crooked, narrow streets past stone houses. If a carriage passed, its wheels might be gilded with miniature, gold foliage or its doors adorned by a painted pastoral scene. Immediately people would give way, scattering to the sides of the road. There were two-wheeled carts pushed by laborers, laundresses with heavy baskets, beggars, fine gentleman with silver-headed canes, blacks and mulattoes, prostitutes and pimps, carpenters, clerks, fishmongers, and

A 1763 illustration of a Caribbean sugar plantation as it would have looked in Hamilton's youth

Slaves at a market being examined before purchase

shopkeepers. There were stray cats and barking mongrel dogs, their bones showing, and barefoot slave children, bones showing too. At Charlestown's slave market Africans were herded together before being drawn out one by one and brought to the auction block. Hamilton witnessed this, as well as slave mistreatment, an everyday, ubiquitous fact of life. Slavery was undoubtedly abhorrent to him then. It always would be.

The West Indies imported 1.2 million slaves between 1700 and 1775.[7] In Nevis, during Hamilton's youth, there were eight Africans for every white inhabitant, some eight thousand slaves altogether.[8] Most were found on the sugar plantations, their treatment beyond imagining. Weakened by tropical diseases and beatings, underfed and rudely sheltered, they labored for twelve or more hours daily. They chopped the ground with hoes at planting or set the leafy tops of the sugarcane aflame at harvest so excess brush did not impede the cutting. Then the strongest slaves, an army of them, took to the fields. Wielding sharp machetes, they slashed at the cane with a fierce, repeated downward sweep of the arm—an athletic feat that would leave a fit but ordinary man "reduced to a standstill within twenty minutes, bent double and soaked with sweat."[9] The work of processing followed. In a plantation's wind-powered mill, as sugarcane was turned to syrup, the slaves stirred the contents of huge boiling vats for hours on end, day and night.

Slaves on plantations in mainland colonies to the north, though suffering cruelly, lived longer than those in the West Indies. In his treatise, *The Groans of the Plantations*, a planter by the name of Edward Littleton advised others on the expected, terrific mortality rates: "He that hath but a hundred *Negroes*, should buy eight or ten every year to keep up his stock."[10] The continual buying of captured humans was a profitable enterprise and inextricably linked to the production of sugar. Both propelled trade and mercantilism; beyond the two, little else sustained wealth in the islands.

Slaves lamenting their fate as they are sent aboard a slave ship

Shipping docks at St. Croix

In 1765, when he was ten, Alexander Hamilton left Nevis with his family and moved to St. Croix, the island his mother had lived on before escaping from Johann Lavien. His father's spotty employment took them there, but he did not stumble upon some more promising universe. Here too slaves and sugar buttressed an economy that, for all its surface glory, could crumble if other sugar-producing locales flooded the market. Again a small number of individuals made unheard-of fortunes while the majority was marginalized. Even though this system cried out for change, a rigid, tenacious, and unyielding system of governance impeded it. Alexander, for his part, could not yet put these pieces together, but in some embryonic way, he noted their existence. Slavery, a monolithic economy, and the injustices of a plutocratic society would be on his mind at a future time and elsewhere, when a new and republican government was under construction.

# "FUTURITY"

Throughout Alexander's childhood, the Hamilton family fortunes were uncertain and James anything but a reliable provider—"My father's affairs at a very early day went to wreck," Hamilton later noted.[11] When James's job in St. Croix ended, he received his pay and unexpectedly departed, deserting his family entirely. We do not know why, but Alexander would never see his father again. The only relationship they maintained was paper-thin, quite literally, contained as it was in a sporadic exchange of letters.

Suddenly Rachel Fawcett was the sole provider for two sons, James, now thirteen, and Alexander, who had just turned eleven. No longer could she turn to her sister, Ann, and brother-in-law, James Lytton—once prosperous, their fortunes had faltered, necessitating the sale of their plantation. Left to her own devices, Rachel proved resourceful. She opened a shop that supplied necessities planters depended on. She purchased both from her landlord and from a counting house run by David Beekman and Nicholas Cruger, two merchants from New York. Cruger probably met Alexander in Rachel's shop. Perhaps he found him bent over the store's ledger, competently totaling up figures. In any case Cruger hired him on, starting as an errand boy and later as a clerk.[12]

Nicholas Cruger, who played a significant role in Hamilton's young life

Life was far from easy during this interval, but it was not without promise when two years along, the family's forward march was interrupted by a series of cataclysms. In January 1768 Rachel was afflicted by a deadly fever. When Alexander also contracted it, he joined her in the one upstairs bed. A doctor provided grim eighteenth-century treatments. The bloodletting and purgatives and emetics produced blood loss, diarrhea, and vomiting. Rachel died. Alexander survived, and the very next day he attended his mother's burial at the sugar plantation once owned by his aunt Ann and uncle James.

Peter Lytton, cousin to James and Alexander Hamilton, was appointed their guardian. A year and half later, he committed suicide and left all he owned to a child he had with his black mistress. One month after that, their uncle James Lytton perished and the boys were not mentioned in his will either.

Nor did James and Alexander receive a penny from their mother's estate. Johann Lavien reappeared and claimed all that Rachel owned for her oldest son, Peter Lavien, whom Johann had sired. By then fully grown and living in South Carolina, Peter was financially solvent. Bent as always on revenge, Lavien gave to his own son what he did not require and purposely left the Hamilton sons destitute.

Gradually the situation improved. James went off to live with a carpenter who employed him. A well-to-do merchant family, the Stevens, took Alexander in. Their attention seemed unwarranted, unless one credits the assertion—based in large part on Alexander's uncanny resemblance in appearance and temperament to the Stevens's son Edward—that he was actually Thomas Stevens' son. If that were true, there had to have been an adulterous relationship between Rachel and the good-hearted Thomas Stevens when she lived on St. Croix with the cold-hearted Johann Lavien. It is conceivable but no proof exists. It's also probable that

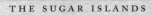

*Dear Edward*                                    *St Croix Novemr 11th 1769*

*This just serves to acknowledge receipt of yours pr Capt Lowndes which was deliverd me yesterday, the truth of Capt Lightbourn & Lowndes information is now verifyd by the Presence of your Father and I...letter, for whose safe arrival I Pray, and that they may convey that Satisfaction to your Soul that must naturally flow from the sight of Absent Friends in health, and shall soon with the way refer you to them, what you say respecting yours, having soon the happiness of seeing us all I wish, for an accomplishment of your hopes provided they are Concomitant with your welfare, otherwise not, tho doubt whether I shall be Present or not, forto confess my weakness, Ned, my Ambition is prevalent that I contemn the Groveling condition of a Clerk or the like, to which my Fortune &c condemns, me and would willingly risk my life tho, not my Character to exalt my Station, I'm confident, Ned that my Youth excludes me from any hopes of immediate Preferment nor do I desire it, but I mean to prepare the way for futurity, I'm no Philosopher you see and may be justly said to Build Castles in the Air, my Folly makes me asham'd and beg you'll Conceal it, yet Neddy we have seen such Schemes successfull when the Projector is Constant I shall Conclude saying I wish there was a War. I am*

*D. Edward.*

*PS*

*This moment Receiv'd yours by William Smith and am pleas'd to see you Give such Close Application to Study*

*Yours*

*Alexr Hamilton*

A 1769 letter from Hamilton to his childhood friend, Edward Stevens

Alexander Hamilton simply attracted Stevens's attention. He was preco-
cious, determined, and competent beyond his years. Nicholas Cruger had
noticed this and willingly assisted him. Stevens might have as well.

By November 1769 Edward Stevens, the son Alexander so resembled,
was at school on the mainland of North America. Alexander, who wanted
no more of a clerk's *grov'ling*, wrote to him: "To confess my weakness,
Ned, my Ambition is prevalent that I contemn the grov'ling and condition
of a Clerk or the like, to which my Fortune &c. condemns me. . . . I mean
to prepare the way for futurity. . . . I'm no philosopher, you see, and may
be jus[t]ly said to build castles in the air, . . . yet Neddy we have seen such
schemes successful when the projector is constant."[13]

Alexander certainly had ambition, and he was indeed constant in
pursuing his *schemes*. Two years later, when Cruger left for a five-month
stint in New York, sixteen-year-old Alexander managed the day-to-day,
nuts-and-bolts operations of his trading company. Apparently, he could
already command stevedores or confront ship captains, and he grasped the
fine points of purchases, sales, inventory, record keeping, shipping routes,
international currency, and exchange rates.

If Hamilton by then had prepared "the way for futurity," good fortune also lent a hand. Fortune arrived oddly packaged in 1772, thanks to
a hurricane that raged for six hours during the last night of August. The
harbor's waves reached to the dark sky and came crashing down on the
boats anchored there. Structures of every size were torn to pieces. Cane
fields were leveled. Appalled by the devastation, Alexander Hamilton wrote
his father a fevered description: "The prodigious glare of almost perpetual
lightning, the crash of the falling houses, and the ear-piercing shrieks of the
distressed, were sufficient to strike astonishment into Angels."[14] Description turned to sermonizing about man's impotence before a vengeful God.
Already Hamilton, who in a lifetime would turn out thousands of pages,

Portrait of Hamilton at age 15

knew how to take command of the page, sending forth a battalion of words. Another of Hamilton's advocates, a minister and journalist named Hugh Knox, read what the boy wrote and determined that it should be published in the newspaper. In a preface, Knox introduced the writer as a "youth of this island." Readers were enamored. Hamilton's champions determined to send the celebrated youngster off to North America for the education he so obviously merited. In all likelihood, Hugh Knox, Nicholas Cruger, and Thomas Stevens were among those who contributed funds to the cause.

Within the year Alexander left the West Indies, never to revisit it and never, publicly, to recollect it fondly. To Neddy Stevens he had admitted to building "castles in the air," and now they were both in a new world— North America—where such dreams were in reach.

# 1773–1777

# An Immigrant Rises

ALEXANDER HAMILTON ESCAPED A SOCIETY THAT WAS FIXED IN PLACE and arrived in one swept by a revolutionary storm of unrest. In the storm's wake, people erected edifices that replaced what had tumbled down, and Hamilton numbered in their company. Luck is in the timing it is said, and Hamilton arrived in time, a few years after one iconic event, the Boston Massacre, and shortly before another, the Boston Tea Party. Within three years of Hamilton's appearing on the scene, British colonists would declare themselves Americans.

## A QUICK STUDY

It was not only timing. At every possible juncture in his young life, Hamilton had prepared for "futurity," as he told Edward Stevens, the

**OPPOSITE:** The first meeting of George Washington (left) and Hamilton

"Neddy" in the letter he wrote at fourteen. When it came, he was primed. Prophetic words had closed the missive: "I shall Conclude saying I wish there was a War."[1] In the eighteenth century, males who lacked opportunity at birth could make their mark and ascend in wartime, a fact Hamilton had assimilated by this early age. Four years later, on the brink of manhood, he was in a new country, and two years after that blood was shed at Lexington and Concord.

In 1773, when Hamilton first appeared in the country on which he would make his mark, he was a boy still in his teens, looking much like any other. First off, he had to make up for deficiencies in a scattershot education that prevented his applying to college. He settled for a time in Elizabeth-town, New Jersey. It was a startlingly new domain for the island-reared

Hamilton, featuring orchards, long meadows, sweeping vistas, and a twisting river shaded by large-limbed elm and poplar trees. In winter the river froze and horses cut their way through snowdrifts. By day Hamilton attended a respected preparatory academy. At night he read late, candles sputtering. Mornings, when walking toward school, he rehearsed the night's lessons by whispering them to himself, seeming to onlookers a bit mad.

Not all was study and tedium during this interlude. Hugh Knox's letters of introduction paved Hamilton's way into a privileged sphere where the St. Croix celebrity met men of the "upper sort," to use the term of the times. One was William Livingston, who occupied Liberty Hall, a

New York as seen from the Hudson River, 1775

Livingston Mansion in Elizabethtown

fine two-story Georgian home set on a 120-acre estate with splendid gardens. At soirees there, Hamilton made a good impression with his attentive azure eyes and acute perceptions. Though he might have felt somewhat out of his element, he was enough at ease to flirt with Livingston's daughter, Kitty. Taken with this intrepid and handsome newcomer, she flirted back.

No doubt Hamilton heard Livingston and those who gathered in his parlour speak heatedly about imperial impingements on colonial rights, such as taxation without representation in Parliament. They opposed absolutism in government and thought of themselves as patriots. Simultaneously, they considered themselves Englishmen and heirs to freedoms and protections that few in the world possessed. As a class, many benefited because the monarch they honored happened to rule a trading empire. The increasing social turmoil discomfited many gentlemen like these. They wondered where it all might lead. The so-called "body of the people" tested the rules and directed the course of action. Included in their numbers were men of the "lower sort"—the rough seamen or untutored laborers and apprentices, who especially rattled those in an upper social sphere. Gouverneur Morris, whose family owned much of the present-day Bronx and who would write the final draft of the new nation's Constitution, made a prediction: "The mob begins to think, and to reason. Poor reptiles! It is with them a vernal morning; they are struggling to cast off their winter's slough [skin], they bask in sunshine, and ere noon they will bite. The gentry begin to fear this. . . . I see, and I see it with fear and trembling, that if the disputes with *Great Britain* continue, we shall be under the worst of all possible dominions; we shall be under the domination of a riotous mob."[2]

After less than a year at the academy Hamilton was more than ready to move on. He applied first to the College of New Jersey, today's Princeton, which his mentor Hugh Knox had attended. Hamilton breezed through his oral examination and then, with marked self-confidence, asked that he be allowed to advance at an accelerated rate. His request was turned down because it was "contrary to the usage of the College."[3] This was not entirely correct. Aaron Burr, whose deceased father had been the college's president, had been allowed to pass through quickly. One rejection did not deter Hamilton from asking King's College in New York for the same favor. They complied.

In New York Hamilton encountered Morris's "reptiles" and also men of "the middling sort," such as craftsmen, shopkeepers, clergymen, printers, and engravers. He even may have lived for a time with the tailor Hercules Mulligan in the rooms above his shop. "Mr. H. used in the evenings to sit with my family and my brother's family and write doggerel rhymes for their amusement," Mulligan said.[4] He was as at home here as at Livingston's Liberty Hall.

New York at the time was a commercial metropolis on the southern tip of Manhattan Island, populated by slightly less than twenty-five thousand people. The city was tailor-made for the youth, who had recorded complex, international trade agreements in Nicholas Cruger's mercantile establishment. Its bustling commerce was in large measure due to ties with the West Indies, where sugarcane occupied every available inch of land, leaving no room for livestock, grain, oats, or barley, and no time for manufacture either. An island's very prosperity left it depleted, and others had to provide foodstuffs, turpentine, pitch, tar, leather, barrels, and other necessities. Half the ships that left New York's harbor sailed to the West Indies with required items. They returned with sugar, ginger, cotton, rum, cocoa, pimento, salt, or lime juice, along with extraordinary quantities of molasses that distillers made into rum.[5]

King's College, soon-to-be Columbia, was located near what was then the city's northern edge, proximate to today's World Trade Center. To the south were the river's newly developed docks and wharves, and to the north, above the last of the city's houses, were pleasure gardens that offered shaded walks, ice cream, and concerts. Beyond were ten miles of farmland and scattered woods, stretching to the northern tip of the island. A high fence surrounded the college grounds and was meant to keep a less scholarly world at bay. Just on the other side a red-light district loomed, and one block away was the Common, where all types gathered by a liberty pole. Over the years New York's Sons of Liberty had stuck these tall, mast-like poles in the ground there and tussled with the British troops trying to topple them. Hamilton's newfound friend Hercules Mulligan was one of those who did battle. Speakers preached insurrectionist gospel on this spot.

Myles Cooper, the president of King's College, subscribed to an entirely different gospel, derived from Greek and Latin scholarship, conservative Tory ideology, and Anglicanism, Britain's established and ceremonious religion. Three men, including Cooper, instructed some twenty students, among them Edward Stevens, who had lived under the

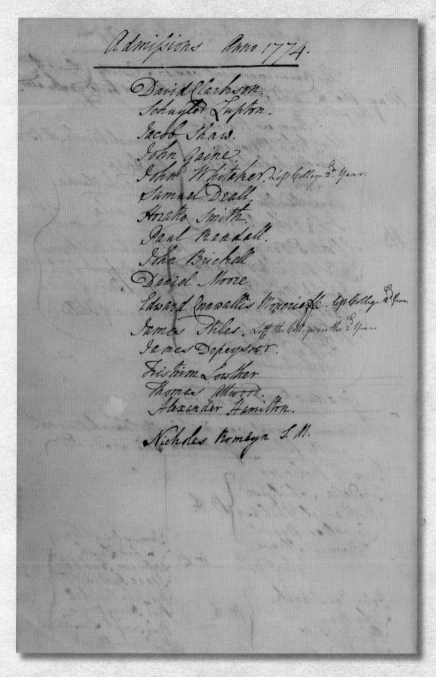

List of students admitted into King's College in 1774; Hamilton is second from the bottom.

same roof as Alexander on St. Croix. Again they were in constant company and Hamilton discovered strong new friendships, like that with Robert Troup, the son of a sea captain who was his roommate and a friend for all his life. The young scholars staged debates and critiqued each other's writing. They rehearsed skills Hamilton would perfect.

## "Who is to Pay the Fiddler?"

On the cold, wet night of December 16, 1773, in a carefully staged act of defiance, companies of men hauled chests of tea from the holds of three British ships, split them apart with hatchets, and tossed the tea leaves into Boston's harbor. The next morning the British admiral John Montagu stood on Griffin's Wharf, fuming at the evidence of destruction. Again and again he cast an angry question at men who passed by—"Who is to pay the fiddler?"[6]

The Province of Massachusetts would, Parliament decreed. In a series of laws it called "Coercive Acts," it closed the Port of Boston and revoked the province's charter. Town meetings were outlawed. The elected council gave way to one appointed by the Crown. As Prime Minister Lord North explained, the idea was to "take the executive power from the hands of the democratic part of the government."[7]

People rebelled throughout Massachusetts. Armed militiamen prevented courts from meeting. Mobs forced the resignation of Crown appointees or forced them to flee to Boston, where British soldiers could protect them. Citizens called town meetings with ever-increasing frequency, just to prove they could. In the end they brought the royal government to a complete standstill. They then began to govern themselves through extralegal bodies. The Empire's restive subjects collected taxes and amassed armaments.

Colonials in New York and elsewhere responded to the escalating crisis of 1774. Militants proposed that Britain pay the fiddler—colonials would not buy British goods until the Coercive Acts were withdrawn. The Sons of Liberty called for a July 6 rally on the Commons near King's College to promote the boycott. Hamilton came and at one point stepped forth to deliver a speech that brought on thundering applause, or so the oft-told tale goes—the historical record provides no documentation.[8] True or not, the story readily took hold because it was so like a thing Hamilton would do. What lay on the other side of any opening was possibility, and when Hamilton spied an opening, he inevitably slipped through. He was not one to stand idly by while others talked and acted.

In September 1774 delegates from twelve states gathered in a Continental Congress at Philadelphia to coordinate resistance. The Congress petitioned the king for redress, to no avail. To force the issue, on October 14 the Congress announced a suspension of all trade with Britain. No goods would come into America, so the prized colonial wheat, tobacco, and rice would shortly be unavailable in the mother country. In the past, prosecution of those who ignored a compact like this was haphazard. But now the Congress called for locally appointed enforcement committees, known soon enough and everywhere as simply the "Association."

In each locale the Association's appointed affiliates had their assignment: "attentively to observe the conduct of all personals touching this association." They spied out violations, and the names of proven violators were "published in the gazette." This could spell ruin in tight-knit communities, and ruin was intended: "All such foes to the rights of British-America may be publicly known, and universally contemned as the enemies of American liberty; and thenceforth we respectively will break off all dealings with him or her." Ostracism was a deadly retribution, a social guillotine.[9]

## SHARP WORDS

Such heavy-handed treatment offended those who looked more favorably on the mother country. In a pamphlet called *Free Thoughts on the Proceedings of the Continental Congress*, Samuel Seabury, a Westchester Anglican clergyman writing under the guise of "A Farmer," went on the attack. "Hear me for I Will speak!" he cried out on the title page. Inside he furiously wrote, "The labour of the congress produced . . . a venomous brood of scorpions, to sting us to death."[10]

Seabury would not go unanswered. "A Friend of America" rebutted "A Farmer" in a scathing thirty-five-page pamphlet entitled *A Full Vindication of the Measures of the Congress, from the Calumnies of their Enemies, in Answer to a Letter, Under the Signature of A. W. Farmer: Whereby his Sophistry is exposed, his Cavils confuted, his Artifices detected, and His wit ridiculed*. When "A Farmer" fired back, "A Friend of America" escalated the war of words with an eighty-five-page manifesto, *The Farmer Refuted*, that probed deeply into every corner of the subject, traveling eloquently from point to point. Following close on the heels of that endeavor were two long letters to the press signed "By the Author of The Farmer Refuted, &c." These targeted Parliament's Quebec Act, which placed all of Quebec under direct rule of the Crown and established Catholicism as the official religion.[11]

Who was this "Friend of America"? Readers assumed he must have been some seasoned and highly educated essayist, perhaps one of the Livingston clan. Myles Cooper, Hamilton's teacher, insisted it was John Jay, a delegate to the Continental Congress who had graduated from King's College eleven years past and who would go on to become the nation's first chief justice of the Supreme Court.[12] Cooper never suspected that it

OPPOSITE: Hamilton was only seventeen when he penned this withering, erudite political broadside

Hamilton, Alexander, 1757-1804

# A
# FULL VINDICATION
OF THE
## Meaſures of the Congreſs,
FROM
The CALUMNIES of their ENEMIES;
IN ANSWER TO
# A LETTER,
Under the Signature of
## A. W. FARMER.
WHEREBY

His *Sophiſtry* is expoſed, his *Cavils* confuted, his *Artifices* detected, and his *Wit* ridiculed;
IN
## A GENERAL ADDRESS
To the *Inhabitants of America,*
AND
## A Particular Addreſs
*To the* FARMERS *of the Province of New-York.*

---

*Veritas magna eſt & prævalebit.*
Truth is powerful, and will prevail.

---

N E W - Y O R K:
Printed by JAMES RIVINGTON. 1774.

was his current student, a recent immigrant just out of his teens, who had actually composed phrases like: "There must be an end of all liberty, where the Prince is possessed of such an exorbitant prerogative, as enables him, at pleasure, to establish the most iniquitous, cruel, and oppressive courts of criminal, civil, and ecclesiastical jurisdiction" and so on.[13]

# REVOLUTION

April 19, 1775, marked a turning point. Britain was not about to let rebellious Massachusetts slip out of its imperial grasp. Urged on by the Crown, the governor of the colony, Thomas Gage, decided to seize armaments and stores that provincials had amassed in Concord. He deployed 800 soldiers who marched through the night and arrived as dawn broke on the village green in Lexington, which lay on their route to Concord. There, about half of the 141 men listed on the town's militia roll were mustering, dressed in everyday coats, waistcoats, and breeches. As the British drew near, one side or the other fired a first shot—no one knows which for sure. As if it were a signal, the redcoats charged. Eight militiamen died in the fray, one pierced by a bayonet.

Regrouping, the king's soldiers continued to Concord. There, in a reversal, militia companies fired on a company of light infantrymen who were guarding the North Bridge. They ran, and within hours the entire British force was retreating toward Boston and coming under persistent fire from patriots who had trained for six months for just such an event. Sixty-five regulars were killed and 180 wounded.

War had begun. There was no going back. Tories everywhere now had to contend with the wrath of patriots. In New York City a handbill targeted Myles Cooper and several others; supposedly the deaths at Lexington and Concord lay at their feet. Coming after Cooper, a mob

GENERAL the HON<sup>ble</sup> THO<sup>s</sup> GAC
OB<sup>t</sup> 1788

ABOVE: John Singleton Copley's portrait of General Thomas Gage, c. 1788
FOLLOWING: Militiamen fall on the Lexington Green

stormed the gates of King's College. That night Hamilton preachified on the stoop of Cooper's quarters to keep them at bay. No matter the politics, he despised the sight of a horde descending on its victim. Then the contest was no contest at all. There was no honor in it. By the next morning, having escaped the vigilantes, Cooper was on a ship bound for England.[14]

Hamilton also sprang to the defense of James Rivington, a Tory printer whose shop was sabotaged by a mob. "Though I am fully sensible how dangerous and pernicious Rivington's press has been, and how detestable the character of the man is in every respect, yet I cannot help disapproving and condemning this step," he reported to John Jay, hoping that Congress could somehow "procure a remedy." The "unthinking populace," he wrote, "who have not a sufficient stock of reason and knowlege to guide them, . . . grow giddy and are apt more or less to run into anarchy."[15] The purpose of a revolution, for Hamilton, was not to destroy all authority but rather to prevent its abuse.

With fellow students and others of his age, temperament, and persuasion, Hamilton volunteered for the militia and drilled daily in a nearby churchyard. But he did more than drill. In any spare moment he paged through books on tactical strategies and military operations.

This powder horn was carved for Reuben Horn by his brother Leonard while he was stationed at Fort Miller in September of 1758. Reuben later responded to the alarm at Lexington and Concord of April 19, 1775 and fought during the beginning of the American Revolution.

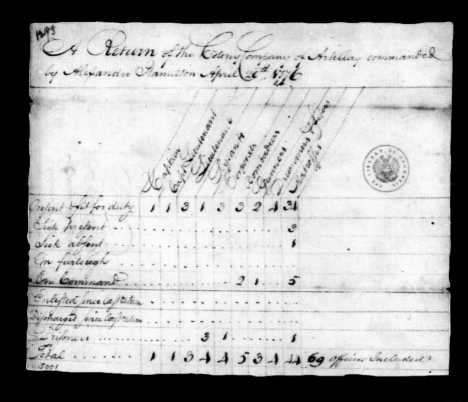

ABOVE: An artillery company report from Hamilton, dated April 20, 1776

BELOW: A powder horn that is believed to have been owned and carried by Alexander Hamilton during his military service in 1776

Alexander Hamilton on the steps of King's College addressing the crowd on the cause of liberty in 1775

While most volunteers were satisfied with muskets, he opted for artillery, seeking instruction from a seasoned soldier. In time he learned how to master the capricious field cannon, whose aim was uncertain, their shells often overshooting a target or falling short. Once more he prepared for "futurity," and he apparently did not imagine himself as only one more soldier in a line of marching men.

At age fourteen Hamilton had written to Neddy Stevens from St. Croix and closed the missive declaring, "I wish there was a war."[16] Even at that early age he realized that a man who lacked wealth or ancestry might make his mark in wartime. That was even more true in his new country. The American military was not the reserve of an aristocratic class as in Europe. In the militia companies that the Continental Army eventually subsumed, a well-regarded blacksmith or farmer could be found drilling a company or leading a charge through the woods. Afterwards, some of these common soldiers received commissions in the Continental Army, where merit could outdistance social rank if one were lucky and had enough backbone, intelligence, and spirit.

In late August 1775, Hamilton showed backbone. At the time, a British man-of-war, the *Asia*, was patrolling New York's waters. Officials feared that cannon in the Battery might come under attack and ordered the Corsicans, a King's College drill company, to remove them. Out the militiamen went on a particularly dark night, when a crescent moon would not rise until just before dawn. Hercules Mulligan later told the tale:

> I recollect well that Mr. Hamilton was there, for I was engaged in hauling off one of the Cannons when Mr. H. came up and gave me his musket to hold, & he took hold of the rope. The punt [a flat-bottomed boat] of the *Asia* had before approached the battery and was fired upon and

a man was killed. She returned to the ship and the fire was then opened upon us. Hamilton at the first firing was away with the Cannon. I left his musket in the Battery and retreated as he was returning. I met him and he asked for his piece. I told him where I had left it, and he went for it, notwithstanding the firing continued, with as much unconcern as if the vessel had not been there.[17]

Through the summer and fall of 1775 a makeshift Continental Army, under the command of Virginia's George Washington, surrounded British forces in Boston. In March 1776, giving up on Massachusetts, the British finally withdrew. Washington guessed correctly where the enemy would likely strike next: New York City, gateway to the Hudson Valley and much of the interior.

Just then, on March 14, the New York Provincial Congress, in preparation for a defense should the British invade, appointed twenty-one-year-old Alexander Hamilton as the leader of an artillery company. The Continental Army had several such companies, but Captain Hamilton's was New York's first. Although younger than most of his sixty-eight gunners and bombardiers, he quickly gained their regard. If he required immaculate dress, he simultaneously commandeered new buckskin breeches. If he insisted on discipline, he also petitioned for, and received, improved pay and rations. What he lacked in experience, he made up for with a surfeit of military know-how and a keen intuition.

For three months, everywhere in New York, untrained soldiers constructed earthworks and prepared for a defensive battle while civilians

OPPOSITE: Drawing of Alexander Hamilton as Captain of Provinicial Company New York Artillery, 1776

FOLLOWING: Map showing Continental Army defences on Manhattan and surrounding area in 1776

D.W.C.Falls
1923

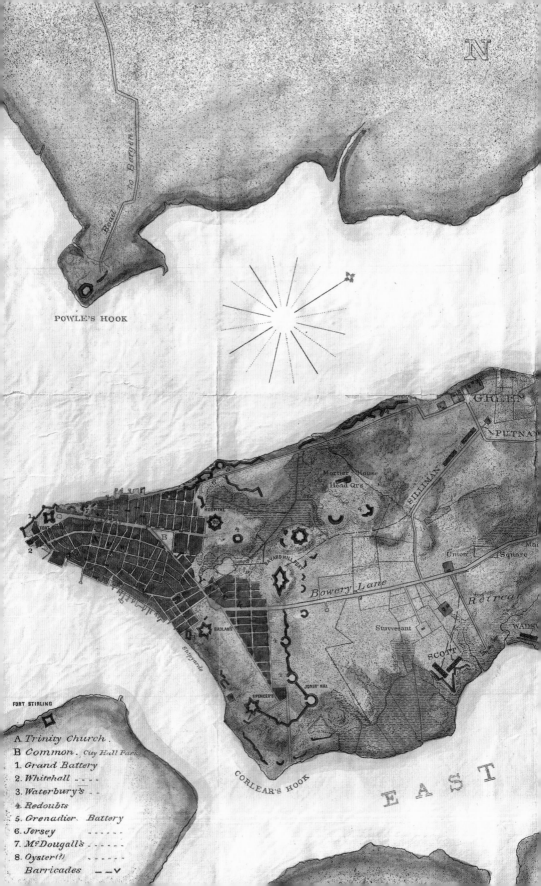

N

POWLE'S HOOK

*Road to Bergen*

FORT STIRLING

A *Trinity Church* .
B *Common* . *City Hall Park* .
1. *Grand Battery*
2. *Whitehall* . . . .
3. *Waterbury's* . .
4. *Redoubts*
5. *Grenadier Battery*
6. *Jersey* . . . . . .
7. *McDougall's* . . . . . .
8. *Oyster(?)* . . . . . .
   *Barricades* . — . . ∨

HOSPITAL

B

BADLAMS

*Shipyards*

SPENCER'S

JONES' HILL

BAYARD HILL FORT

*Bowery Lane*

Mortier House
Head Qrs

SILLIMAN

Stuyvesant

SCOTT

Union Square

*Retreat*

WADS

GREEN

PUTNAM

Mad

CORLEAR'S HOOK

EAST

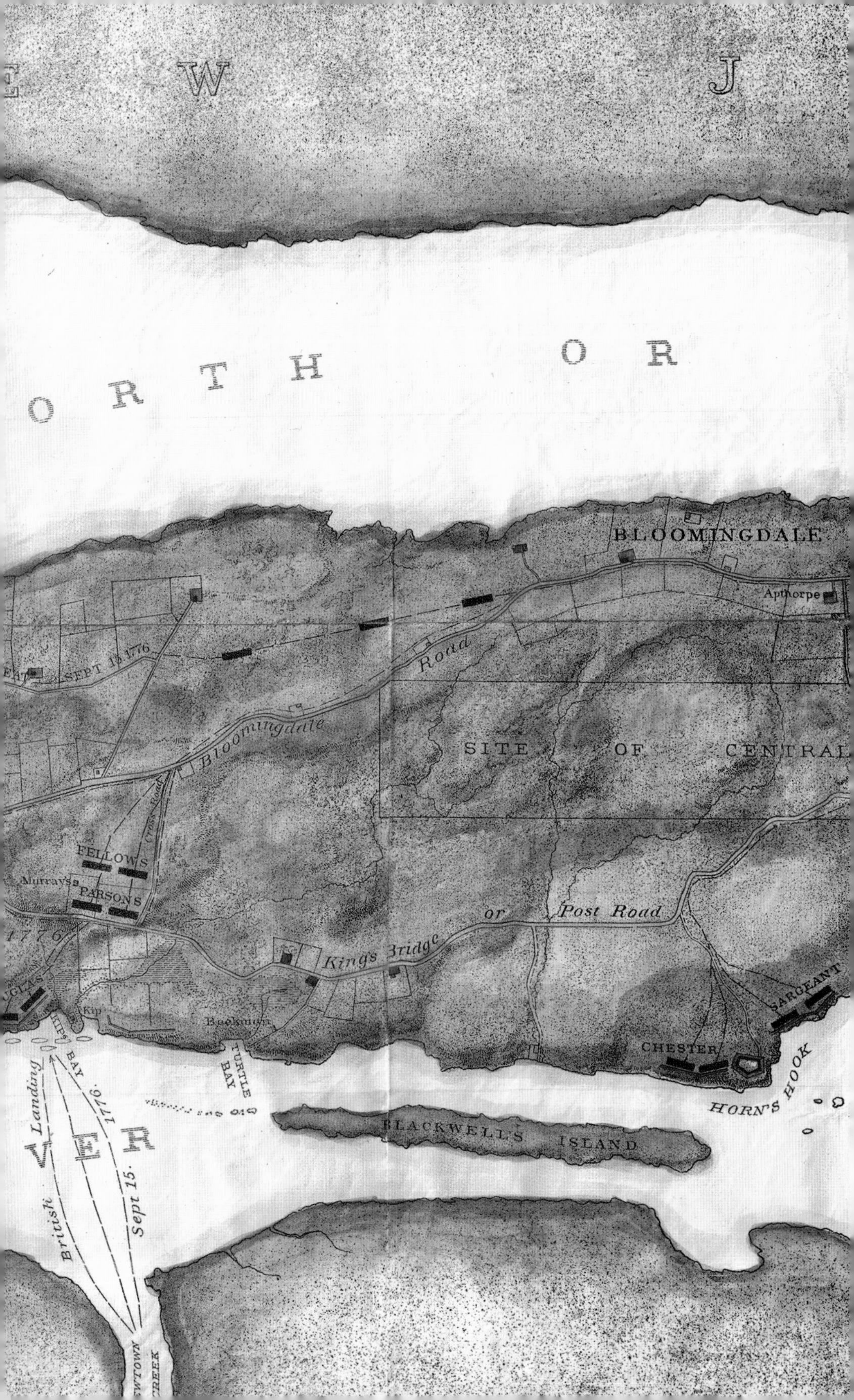

W
J
F

N O R T H    O R

BLOOMINGDALE

Apthorpe

Road

SEPT 15 1776

Bloomingdale

SITE    OF    CENTRAL

FELLOWS

Murray's
PARSONS

or    Post Road

1776

Kings Bridge

DOUGLAS

Kip

SARGEANT

Beekman

CHESTER

HORN'S HOOK

TURTLE
BAY

Landing

SHIP BAY

1776

British

Sept 15. 1776.

V E R

BLACKWELLS ISLAND

EWTOWN

CREEK

abandoned the city. At Bayard's Hill, in today's Little Italy, Hamilton worked alongside his men as they threw up a makeshift fort and installed cannon. Then, late in June and into July, the enemy arrived, the largest armed force ever assembled in the war-filled eighteenth century—23,000 regulars, 9,000 Hessian mercenaries, a few thousand seamen, and 427 seaworthy vessels, both transports and warships, armed with some 1,200 cannon. One New Yorker recorded his first sighting of the masts: "I spied, as I peeped out the Bay, something resembling a Wood of pine trees trimmed . . . I do believe all London was afloat."[18]

British forces gathered first on Staten Island, a post that command-ed the harbor and entrance to the Hudson River. Late in August almost 20,000 men swarmed across Long Island, just to the east of Manhattan. Washington and the bulk of the Continental forces met the British there

ABOVE: The Delaware Regiment fighting the rearguard action at the Battle of Long Island, which allowed the remainder of the Continental Army to escape from advancing British forces. OPPOSITE: Disposition of British and American troops at the start of the Battle of Brooklyn (aka Long Island)

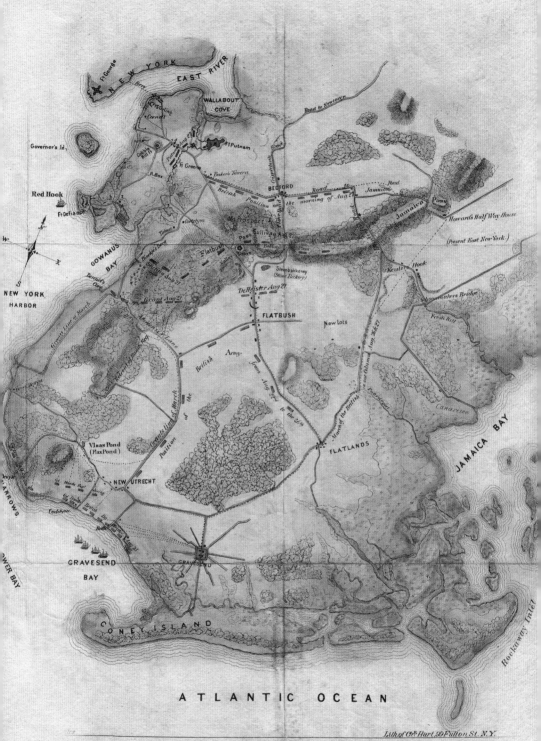

# Plan of the Battle of Brooklyn
### AUGUST 27TH 1776.

but were overwhelmed. Stealthily, in the dead of night, they managed to escape to Manhattan, where Hamilton and others had been preparing a line of defense.

In mid-September, 13,000 British soldiers launched an assault on New York City itself, crossing in waves on flatboats, the tall ships anchored close by "vomiting flames and murderous shot" under "rolling volleys of smoke."[19] The overwhelming force waded ashore at Kips Bay, northeast of Hamilton's Bayard's Hill fortification, cutting his company off as Americans fled up the island toward Harlem Heights. His own retreating men barely made it past the enemy.

That fall, the Americans were forced to retreat from one imagined stronghold to another. They held Harlem, then abandoned it for White Plains. When the British arrived there, Washington led his army across the Hudson River and southward through New Jersey. As the infantry retreated, Hamilton's artillery company held back the pursuing troops. Gunner crews trained by Hamilton fired again and again to keep the British at bay, if only for a few moments or hours. He was no longer a

American forces under General Stirling fleeing across Gowanus Creek in the Battle of Long Island

Continental soldiers evacuating Fort Lee, New Jersey, in November 1776

Emanuel Leutze's iconic 1851 painting *Washington Crossing the Delaware*

militia captain but part of the Continental Army's artillery, commanded by Henry Knox.

The situation was desperate. Embedded with the retreating army, writing when and where he could, Thomas Paine spoke of the "times that try men's souls." "The harder the conflict, the more glorious the triumph. What we obtain too cheap, we esteem too lightly."[20] Washington made sure Paine's words reached his men—he was about to test them.

On Christmas night, Washington sent his army across the Delaware River. The flat-bottomed scows dodged ice floes, and the men huddled on them peered through the sleet, seeing little. By three in the morning infantry and artillery units and horses and cannon had all landed on the far side. As the line approached the Hessian camp in Trenton, a blanket of thick snow dulled the sound of their marching feet and it was the fire from their guns that woke the startled enemy soldiers. According to Knox, they "endeavored to form," but couldn't; "cannon and howitzers . . . in the twinkling of an eye cleared the streets."[21]

One week later, when General Cornwallis arrived from New York with a large force of British regulars, American artillery staved them off for a few hours, until nightfall. Then, using the nighttime dark as a protective

Gilbert Stuart's portrait of Henry Knox

cover once more, Washington moved his forces northward to Princeton and overran a British contingent caught unawares. Record-keeping was the last thing on anybody's mind, but it is likely, if not officially certified, that Hamilton's company was in the thick of the action at Princeton, as it had been at Trenton. The victories reenergized an army, and a nation.

Armies in northern climes rarely undertook winter campaigns. As Cornwallis returned to the British stronghold at New York, Washington and the Continentals established their winter camp forty miles to the east in Morristown, New Jersey.

Hamilton's artillery company in the Battle of Trenton, December 26, 1776

General Charles Cornwallis

# FAMILY

Two weeks after the Battle of Princeton, as the commander in chief took stock of the army's changing personnel, he asked Alexander Hamilton to accept a prestigious appointment as his aide-de-camp. Some later reported that General Nathanael Greene recommended the distinguished young artillery officer; others, that it was Henry Knox. Several claimed that Hamilton won favor because Washington took note of his valor in this battle or that. But Washington thought that valorous, battle-tested men were not so rare as "men of judgment . . . & *ready pens* to execute them properly, & with dispatch."[22] The commander in chief managed a war and an entire, far-flung army and depended on men who could churn out the mass of reports, orders, and letters a war required. Those he valued most had to "possess the Soul of the General and from a *single* Idea given to them, to convey his meaning."[23] In 1776, because Washington's deskwork obliged him "to neglect many other essential parts of my Duty," he had actively recruited but turned down many aspirants. "It is absolutely necessary," he wrote, "for me to have persons that can think for me, as well as execute Orders."[24]

Hamilton's skill set perfectly matched the job description. If Washington needed to cut a corner when pressed for time, he might make the cut and hand the jagged remnant to Hamilton. Adroitly marshaling facts and figures, this aide-de-camp could quickly produce a document that answered exactly to Washington's needs. During Hamilton's service Washington deployed him as horseman, spy, and interpreter, and he

OPPOSITE: Washington at the Battle of Princeton

intermittently applied to him for counsel. He sent him off to negotiate with superior officers who were shocked when such a young man appeared and likely irritated by the underling's audacity. Hamilton was not only a favorite but, before long, a necessity it seemed. He dressed now in a uniform with green ribbons that identified him as an aide-de-camp and sported a lieutenant colonel's gold epaulets on the shoulders of his coat.[25]

As an aide, Hamilton was one of an entourage that George Washington called his "family"—the handpicked men who orbited a commander who was six foot two inches tall, a majestic height in his day. A physician and staunch patriot from Philadelphia, Benjamin Rush, spoke about Washington's "martial dignity," claiming that "there is not a king in Europe that would not look like a valet de chamber by his side."[26] Elizabeth Dyer of Philadelphia seems to have had a similar impression. She put it more plainly—"He seems discrete & Virtuous, no harum Scarum ranting Sweating fellow, but Sober, steady, & Calm."[27]

A life mask made in preparation for a later sculpture shows Washington's high forehead and a long, crooked roman nose, straight and narrow lips, and even the mark of a scar on one cheek. He was powerfully built with broad shoulders and the long legs and muscled thighs of an inveterate horseman, which he was. He dashed his light brown hair with powder. He attracted the respect of the men who served under him in the hectic, workaday military world and from some drew an undying allegiance.

Closeted together, poring over documents with desks set close, sleeping side by side or even two to a bed, exposed to danger, the general's aides formed a tight fraternity. The familial backdrop meant much to a man like Hamilton, who had lost his family. His ties with fellow aides were close. Some were loving and endured far into the future. Now proximate to power at the very highest level, the immigrant from St. Croix was an outsider no longer.

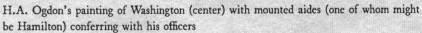

H.A. Ogdon's painting of Washington (center) with mounted aides (one of whom might be Hamilton) conferring with his officers

# IN CONGRESS.

The DELEGATES of the UNITED STATES of *New-Hampſhire, Maſſachuſetts-Bay, Rhode-Iſland, Connecticut, New-York, New-Jerſey, Pennſylvania, Delaware, Maryland, Virginia, North-Carolina, South-Carolina* and *Georgia*, TO

*John Brown Gentᵣ*

WE, repoſing eſpecial Truſt and Confidence in your Patriotiſm, Valour, Conduct and Fidelity, DO, by theſe Preſents, conſtitute and appoint you to be *a Lieutenant in Colᵒ Sheldon's Regᵗ of Light Dragoons to take Rank from the eleventh day of October 1777 Seventy Seven* in the Army of the United States, raiſed for the Defence of American Liberty, and for repelling every hoſtile Invaſion thereof. You are therefore carefully and diligently to diſcharge the Duty of *a Lieutenant* by doing and performing all manner of Things thereunto belonging. And we do ſtrictly charge and require all Officers and Soldiers under your Command, to be obedient to your Orders as *A Lieutenant* And you are to obſerve and follow ſuch Orders and Directions from Time to Time, as you ſhall receive from this or a future Congreſs of the United States, or Committee of Congreſs, for that purpoſe appointed, or Commander in Chief, for the Time being, of the Army of the United States, or any other your ſuperior Officer, according to the Rules and Dicipline of War, in Purſuance of the Truſt repoſed in you. This Commiſſion to continue in Force until revoked by this or a future Congreſs. DATED at *the 1ˢᵗ day of Janᵧ 1778* By Order of the CONGRESS,

Atteſt. *Cha Thomson ſecy* *Henry Laurens*, PRESIDENT.

*Lieut Brown has the Commander in Chief's Permiſſion to reſign his rank in the army of The United States and is hereby discharged from the ſervice By his Excellency's Command Head Quarters New Alex Hamilton Windſor June 22ᵈ 1779 Aid de Camp*

The back of this document appointing John Brown as a lieutenant in Col. Sheldon's Light Dragoons is a discharge paper signed by Hamilton, acting in his role as Washington's aide-de-camp

Hamilton grew particularly close to John Laurens, whose father, Henry Laurens, was the president of the Continental Congress. John Laurens opposed slavery and had viewed its brutal customs close at hand on his family's enormous plantation in South Carolina. "We have sunk the African[s] and their descendants below the standard of humanity,"[28] he wrote. The young Laurens concocted a plan to raise battalions of black slaves who would exchange military service for freedom. Hamilton joined in. In March 1779 he once again lobbied fellow New Yorker John Jay, who by then had succeeded Henry Laurens as president of Congress. "I have not the least doubt that the negroes will make very excellent soldiers. . . . their natural faculties are as good as ours," Hamilton asserted and asked that Congress back John Laurens's scheme.[29] To the alarm of slave masters, Congress proposed that South Carolina and Georgia raise three thousand black troops and put them under the charge of white commanders. In those state legislatures, not surprisingly, the measure failed.

Another prominent aide was the Marquis de Lafayette, a nineteen-year-old French nobleman whose father died in battle during the Seven Years' War when the marquis was two. His mother died when he was eleven, leaving him one of France's largest fortunes. Some years later, in 1775, he attended a dinner party. King George III's younger brother was at the table. The duke railed on and on about the naivety of colonial rebels who touted the equality of mankind and who thought that they could rule themselves effectively. As the duke mocked their Continental Army, Lafayette listened harder. "My heart was enlisted, and I thought only of joining my colors to those of the revolutionaries," he later said.[30]

In 1777 Lafayette sailed to America on the *Victoire*, which he had bought himself after the Continental Congress said they could not afford his transport. French aristocrats, spurred on by romantic republican notions, were arriving in droves. They often expected to take command

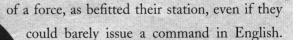

of a force, as befitted their station, even if they could barely issue a command in English. Unlike most, Lafayette already had a rudimentary grasp of English and soon was fluent; he and Hamilton may have conversed in French as well since Hamilton spoke it freely. He not only agreed to serve without pay but drew funds out of his very deep pockets for uniforms and arms. At nineteen, Lafayette was appointed a major general. Years later Hamilton's wife, Eliza, would say that "the marquis loved Mr. Hamilton as a brother; their love was mutual."[31]

Having studied medicine, James McHenry joined the staff. He shared medical advice but also the heroic verses he composed. Hamilton reported they sang together—"He and I are accustomed to regale the ears of the fraternity."[32]

These men bantered, teased, and gave each other nicknames. The combative and bold Alexander Hamilton was "the little lion." Above all, there was camaraderie. They confided in each other. They trusted and depended on each other. In war they were closely bound.

OPPOSITE: 1791 portrait of the Marquis de Lafayette in his lieutenant general's uniform
ABOVE: James McHenry

# III

# 1777–1780

# The Perils of War

In January and February 1777, as men departed after their enlistments ended, Washington's force dwindled to about 2,500 soldiers. Short of men, he adapted and sent Continentals out to fight alongside New Jersey militia companies made up of citizen-soldiers, most of them farmers. Winter was a good time for farmers to campaign, their fields lying fallow, and the militia numbers were vastly higher than Washington's own. If at first he had grumbled that the would-be soldiers answered only to their own leaders and "come and go when they please," now his force worked in tandem with them. They targeted the British Regulars and light infantry and the Hessian dragoons who occupied the New Jersey outposts General Howe had left behind after withdrawing his main force to New York. Since the camps never had enough supplies, men foraged in the countryside for

**OPPOSITE:** Hamilton supervising construction of redoubts at the Siege of Yorktown

what they could find, particularly fodder for the horses that pulled artillery and supply wagons—war would come to a halt if those animals did.

## BRANDYWINE: "WE SHALL BEAT THEM SOUNDLY"

By June the Continental force had swelled to 14,000. Many of the new recruits had no military experience, and it was the so-called *forage wars* that provided their schooling. For the first time they faced a foe, clashing time and again with the king's soldiers during the spring and summer. In a letter to Hugh Knox, Hamilton wrote of "trifling skirmishes" that "served to harass, and waste away the enemy, and teach our own men to look them in the face with confidence."[1] A British colonel, Allan MacLean, spoke in a more acidic tone of British troops having "been tossed and kicked about most amazingly."[2] Hamilton's "trifling skirmishes" took their toll as British losses accumulated. Howe tried to lure Washington into a confrontation on open ground where he could trounce him. The American commander never took the bait.

Finally, on July 23, Howe made a decisive move. The previous December British forces had been within days of seizing Philadelphia, the infant nation's capital. It was then that Washington's small force struck at Trenton and Princeton, disrupting his plan. Again Howe determined to assail the capital, this time with greater force and planning. A fleet of 266 ships put to sea carrying Hessian mercenaries and British regulars along with dragoons, artillery, horses, and supplies. They were to land on the shore of Chesapeake Bay, fifty miles from Philadelphia.

OPPOSITE: *The Nation Makers* by Howard Pyle, 1906, depicting the American infantry at the Battle of Brandywine on September 11, 1777

The proximity of the British seemed to electrify Hamilton. He reported to Gouverneur Morris, now a member of the New York State Assembly, in what seemed a battle cry: "The enemy will have Philadelphia, if they dare make a bold push for it, unless we fight them a pretty general action. I opine we ought to do it, and that we shall beat them soundly if we do. . . . I would not only fight them, but I would attack them; for I hold it an established maxim, that there is three to one in favour of the party attacking."[3]

General Washington took a position at Chadds Ford, a crossing on Brandywine Creek that was directly in the line of the British march. When combat ensued, the rebel army faced a professional one, but even when forced to retreat, Americans rallied again and again. One hill changed hands upwards of five times. General Washington and his "family" were in the thick of it. A private soldier described the horrific scene:

> Cannons roaring muskets cracking drums beating bumbs flying all round. Men a dying wounds horred grones which would greave the heardist of hearts to see such a dollful sight as this to see our fellow creators slain in such a manner.[4]

Here was the "general action" Hamilton wanted. Americans did not beat the British "soundly," as he had predicted, but they did stand up to them, their valor confirmed. Uncharacteristically, Americans did not tabulate their casualties, but British reports estimated that some 1,300

John Laurens

ABOVE: Lafayette wounded trying to rally soldiers during the Battle of Brandywine.
FOLLOWING: An engraved map of the Battle of Brandywine, 1777

were killed, wounded, or taken prisoner. The Marquis de Lafayette was shot in the leg; in his memoir, he recalled hearing Washington's order to the surgeons—"Treat him as though he were my son."[5] After the battle, Lafayette was given command of a division. John Laurens displayed great courage but emerged from the bloody contest unscathed. As Lafayette later reported to Henry Laurens, "It was not his fault that he was not killed or wounded. He did every thing that was necessary to procure one or t'other."[6] This was not what a father might want to hear.

Having failed to thwart the British advance, Washington instead determined to demolish supplies that might fall into enemy hands, a customary tactical maneuver. One detachment's mission was to destroy flour in mills located on the banks of the Schuylkill River. Hamilton,

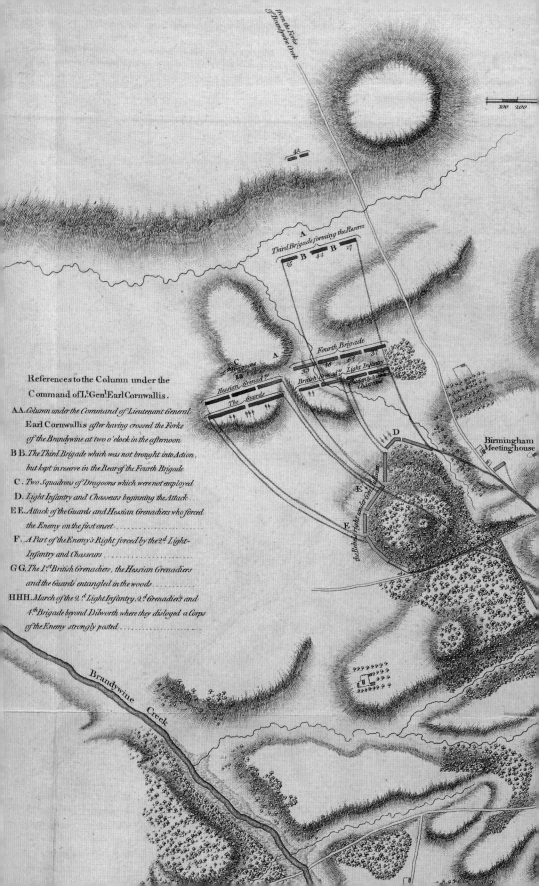

from the Forks
of Brandywine Creek

100    100

A
Third Brigade forming the Reserve
B    44    B
15                    27

Fourth Brigade
C    A    64    31
32    10

2d Squadron    British Grenad.rs    Light Infantry
Hessian Grenad.rs    Hessian & Anspach Chasseurs
The Guards

D

Birmingham
Meeting house

E

The Rebels right wing to Gen.l Washington
E

References to the Column under the
Command of L.t Gen.l Earl Cornwallis.

A A. Column under the Command of Lieutenant General
Earl Cornwallis after having crossed the Forks
of the Brandywine at two o'clock in the afternoon

B B. The Third Brigade which was not brought into Action,
but kept in reserve in the Rear of the Fourth Brigade

C . Two Squadrons of Dragoons which were not employed

D. Light Infantry and Chasseurs beginning the Attack .............

E E. Attack of the Guards and Hessian Grenadiers who forced
the Enemy on the first onset .............

F . A Part of the Enemy's Right forced by the 2.d Light-
Infantry and Chasseurs .............

G G. The 1.st British Grenadiers, the Hessian Grenadiers
and the Guards entangled in the woods .............

H H H. March of the 2.d Light Infantry, 2.d Grenadiers and
4.th Brigade beyond Dilworth where they dislodged a Corps
of the Enemy strongly posted .............

Brandywine

Creek

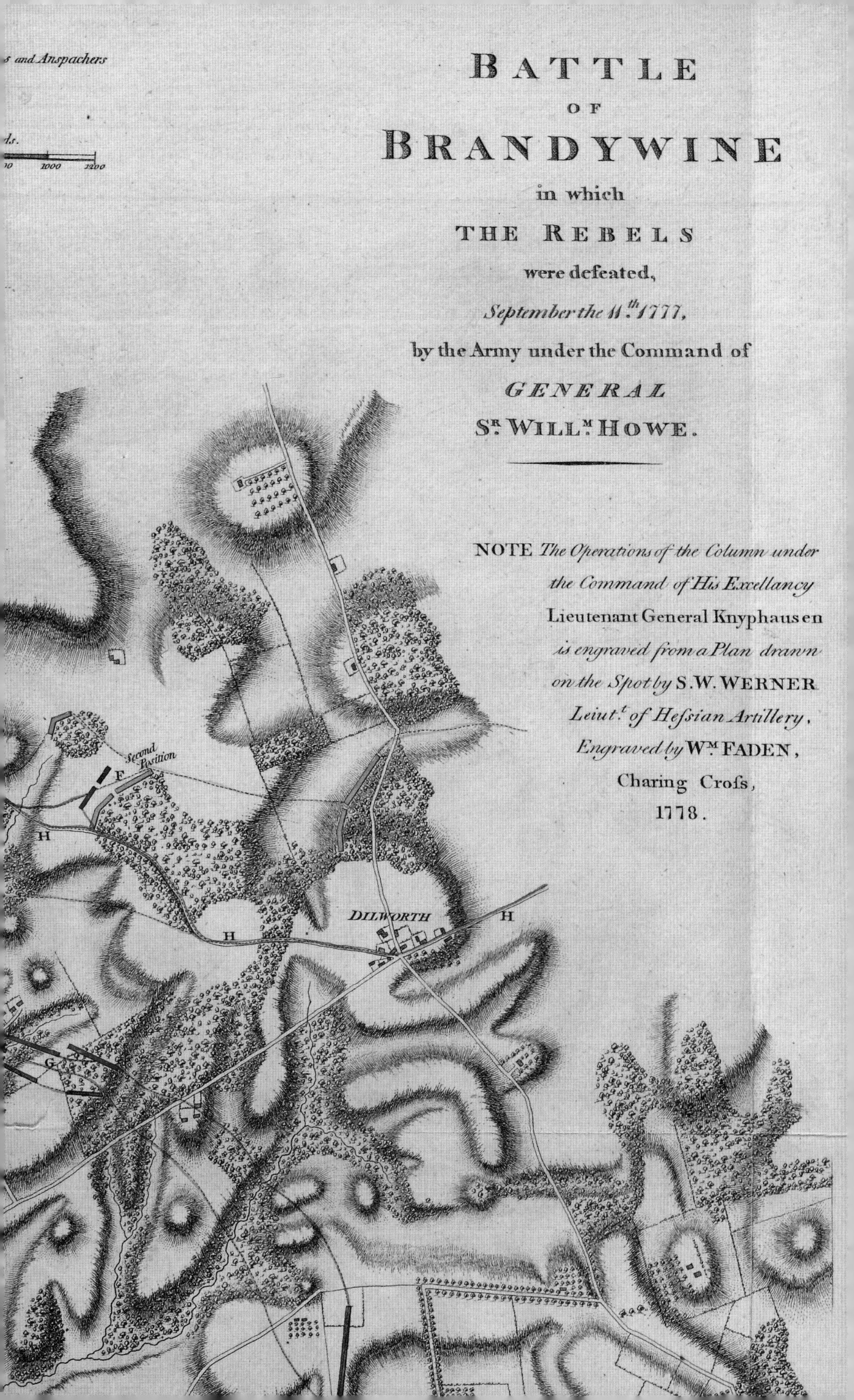

# BATTLE
## OF
# BRANDYWINE
in which
## THE REBELS
were defeated,
September the 11th 1777,
by the Army under the Command of
## GENERAL
## Sr. Willm. HOWE.

NOTE *The Operations of the Column under the Command of His Excellancy Lieutenant General Knyphausen is engraved from a Plan drawn on the Spot by* S.W. WERNER *Lieutt. of Hessian Artillery,* Engraved by Wm. FADEN, Charing Cross, 1778.

s and Anspachers

ds.

2000    2400

Second Position

F

H

H

DILWORTH    H

G

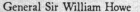

General Sir William Howe

who continually longed for action, was in the company. When British dragoons caught them in the act, some men escaped on horseback while Hamilton and three others pushed off in a boat. Coming under continual fire, they dove into the Schuylkill's raging waters, barely making it to shore, soaked from head to foot and with one man shot. Hamilton steadied himself and quickly drafted a missive to John Hancock, president of the Continental Congress: "If Congress have not yet left Philadelphia, they ought to do it immediately without fail, for the enemy have the means of throwing a party this night into the city."[7] By dawn, losing no time, Congressional delegates had packed their bags and departed to Lancaster, Pennsylvania, out of harm's way.

The British did not actually arrive until September 26, eight days later. In the formidable line of march were Regulars in their smart crimson jackets and dragoons on prancing horses. The plumes on Hessian helmets quivered with each synchronized step. A seeming invincible train of artillery filed past. A tune played—"God Save the King".

General Howe left Philadelphia under the command of Lord Cornwallis and established a bivouac for nine thousand of his soldiers in Germantown, six miles to the northwest. George Washington decided that he would have at the encampment. After Brandywine it was hardly a thing Howe would expect, and surprise, as at Trenton, would itself be a weapon. His men made their way across sixteen miles of thickly wooded territory on the night of October 2. A thick fog, soon intermingling with smoke from musket fire, blanketed everything in sight. At times, soldiers were barely able to see each other, let alone their adversaries. For five hours, attack followed harrowing counterattack. In the end the Continentals drew back, with 152 killed, some 500 wounded, and 438 captured, more than double British casualties.

**ABOVE AND FOLLOWING:** During the Battle of Germantown, British troops seized the home of Benjamin Chew, Chief Justice of Pennsylvania. American attempts to dislodge the British from their impenetrable stronghold resulted in heavy casualties, as these illustrations depict.

# SARATOGA: "THE PALM OF VICTORY"

A potential but yet undecided ally, France, witnessed these events closely. French officials also kept an eye on the progress of the British general John Burgoyne as he advanced in a southward direction through the Champlain Valley from Quebec. He gloated that he would take his Christmas dinner in Albany. Elizabeth Schuyler, Hamilton's future wife, made her home in the threatened city, while General Philip Schuyler, her father, commanded American soldiers who were bent on protecting it. Burgoyne presumed that General Howe would march north along the Hudson River and buttress the campaign he waged, but Howe was occupied elsewhere—once he fastened his sights on General Washington, he never did relent.

Burgoyne's greatest adversary may not have been Schuyler but instead the dense wilderness that impeded his overloaded baggage train. It inched along through forests and over bogs, gaining at times only a mile in a day. Schuyler's men felled trees across Burgoyne's path, took

out bridges, and destroyed provisions he wanted to seize. In Albany, Catherine Schuyler, Philip's wife, anticipated a British assault and set ablaze the fields of grain that might

Portrait of British General John Burgoyne, who advanced in a southward direction through the Champlain Valley from Quebec. He gloated that he would take his Christmas dinner in Albany.

Mrs. Schuyler burning her wheat fields on the approach of the British

fall into their hands. Meanwhile, militiamen by the thousands arrived to strengthen American numbers.

Victory seemed possible when, on August 4, Congress stripped General Schuyler of his command and assigned General Horatio Gates to the post. Boiling with anger, Schuyler wrote to the man replacing him, "The palm of victory is denied me, and it is left to you, General, to reap the

fruits of my labors."[8] When Burgoyne did surrender his army of almost 6,000 men at Saratoga in mid-October, Gates was indeed celebrated across America, although some, like Schuyler beforehand and Alexander Hamilton afterwards, thought that others deserved the credit. The British defeat decided the vacillating French, who pledged long-awaited financial and military support. That was as significant a victory as the military one.

After Saratoga, Washington sent a message to Hamilton: "It having been judged expedient by the members of a Council of War held Yesterday, that one of the Gentlemen of my family should be sent to Genl. Gates . . . to point out to him the many happy consequences that will accrue from an immediate reinforcement being sent from the Northern Army; I have thought proper to appoint you to that duty."[9] The general was enlisting his aide as a courier and, much more than that, as a diplomat. Hamilton was to demand collaboration from a general who didn't readily collaborate. He was to effect the reassignment of troops under Gates's command, a thing that Gates, in his newly glorified state, would find demeaning.

ABOVE: This Massachusetts regimental drum is embellished with the pine tree symbol commonly used during the Revolutionary War. OPPOSITE, TOP: General Arnold wounded in the assault on the Hessian redoubt at the Battle of Saratoga. OPPOSITE, BOTTOM: A military kettle drum belonging to the British Royal Norfolk Regiment, which surrendered to the Continental Army after the Battle of Saratoga

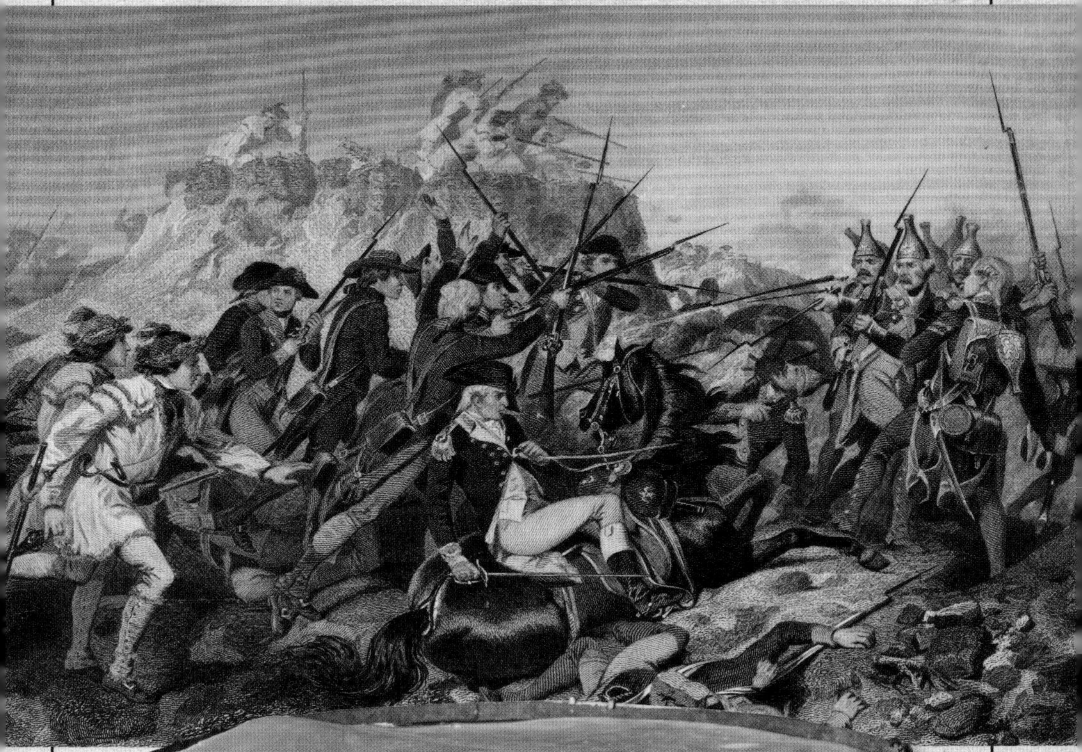

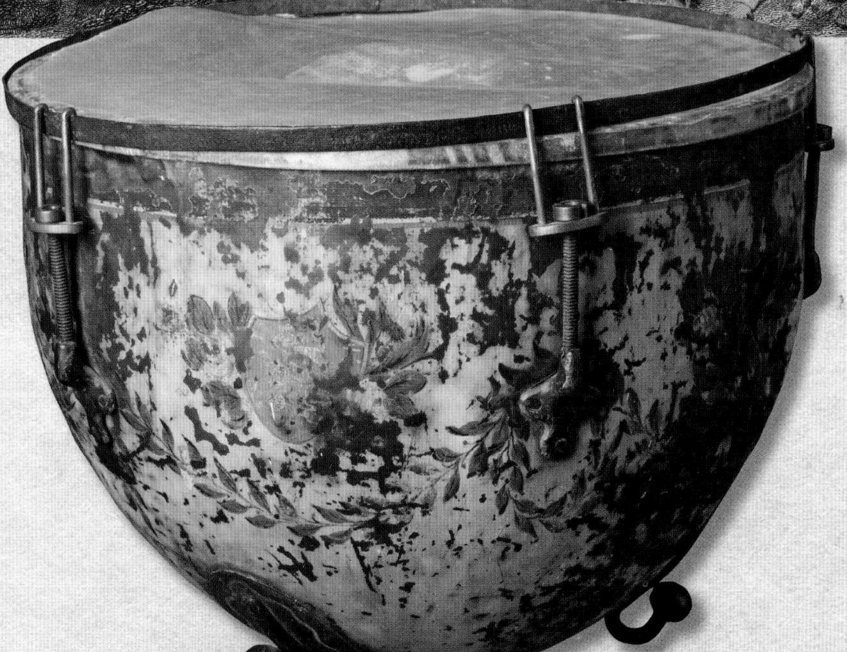

Orders in hand, Hamilton took off for Albany, three hundred miles distant. The autumn light died early, driving him on. Once, on his own initiative, he interrupted the five-day journey to communicate to General Israel Putnam the desperate need for reinforcements from his troops. Then Hamilton was back in the saddle and headed for Albany. Not surprisingly, the confrontation between one general and the aide of another was awkward. Peering through spectacles perched atop a long nose, Gates argued for the transfer of one brigade, not the three that Washington requested. Hamilton pressed the point, and Gates finally agreed to dispatch two. In a letter to Washington, Gates seethed over the encounter and over the intolerably young aide's "dictatorial power."[10]

In Albany Hamilton dined with Philip Schuyler and met the general's family, including his daughter Elizabeth. There is no record of love taking flame, as it would in two years' time. Shortly after his departure from the city, Hamilton's odyssey ended abruptly when he fell deathly ill. Through November and December, as he harbored in one residence or another, chills and fevers racked his body. There were fears he would die. He did not.

OPPOSITE: Continental Army general Horatio Gates. In a letter to Washington, Gates seethed over his encounter with Hamilton and over the intolerably young aide's "dictatorial power." RIGHT: Watercolor painting of Hamilton by Charles Willson Peale

## VALLEY FORGE: SURVIVAL

Hamilton did not make his way to the winter camp at Valley Forge until the end of the third week in January, and when he did arrive he was still weak. It was perhaps not the best place for a man to recover. Typhus, typhoid, dysentery, and influenza ravaged the camp. Soldiers died in droves, some 2,000 in all. All suffered, not so much from the cold—the winter weather was warmer than usual for that locale—but because everything was in short supply. There were not nearly enough rations,

William T. Trego's 1883 painting *Washington Reviewing His Troops at Valley Forge* was inspired by the Nathaniel Hawthorne line: "Sad and dreary was the march to Valley Forge"

coats, breeches, shoes, or blankets. Without fodder, horses were dying; their carcasses littered the ground. Washington pleaded his case with Congress to no avail. Lacking the authority to raise its own funds, Congress depended on money from state governments, but states in turn had difficulty collecting taxes from financially strapped citizens. Hamilton had only to look around him to calculate the human price of such dysfunction.

Washington's Prussian drill master Baron Frederick William August von Steuben

A month after Hamilton arrived in camp, Washington greeted a newcomer to the cause, Baron Frederick William August von Steuben. Bearing a letter of introduction from Benjamin Franklin, the Prussian officer was something to behold in his grand uniform, a glittering medallion hanging from the gold ribbon about his neck. Born into a military family of high standing, Steuben was a godson of Prussia's second king, Friedrich Wilhelm I. Upon coming of age, he entered the military and served directly under Prussia's third king, Frederick the Great. He was a proven combat veteran, but, most importantly, a drillmaster who employed the advanced techniques used in the highly regarded Prussian army.

At Washington's urging, Congress soon made a major general of von Steuben, and through the spring soldiers practiced the exacting tactical maneuvers that he prescribed. Von Steuben sought uniformity. The Continental Army was not without discipline, but men had been drilling under individual regimental commanders. When diverse regiments engaged an enemy in the field, confusion could ensue. Von Steuben trained soldiers in all regiments to march in perfect synchronization, break from their ranks to form a firing line, discharge their muskets in unison, reload quickly, and fire again. Hamilton and John Laurens translated the manual that von Steuben wrote out in French into English, editing as they went along. Called the "Blue Book" because of its blue cover, von Steuben's "Regulations for the Order and Discipline of the Troops of the United States" was distributed to every regiment, reinforcing military protocols within the entire army.

Washington inspecting his troops with Lafayette

While Valley Forge soldiers sought uniformity as they persistently drilled, officers jostled for positions awarded by the Continental Congress. This was customary, but following Saratoga, the jostling intensified. Some even conspired to replace Washington with the now preeminent general, Horatio Gates. One member of the faction opposed to Washington was Thomas Conway, an Irishman who had forged a career in the French army and now sought opportunity in the Continental Army. After proving his worth at Brandywine and Germantown, he vigorously sought and won—against Washington's counsel—a promotion to major general. Congress even appointed him inspector general, in charge of investigating what was wrong within the Continental Army.

The main thing wrong with the army, Conway thought, was its leadership. Writing to General Gates, whom he favored over Washington, he wrote: "What pity there is but one Gates! but the more I see of this Army the less I think it fit for general Action under its actual Chiefs & actual discipline."[11] From within Gates's camp, a distorted version of that letter leaked out: "Heaven has been determined to save your Country, or a weak General and bad Councillors would have ruined it."[12] Washington, the so-called "weak general," went public with the letter, which caused a great stir. And Hamilton, no doubt one of the "bad Councillors," launched an attack—the anti-Washington faction was a "monster," and Conway

This .69 caliber infantry musket was standard issue for American soldiers during the Revolutionary War.

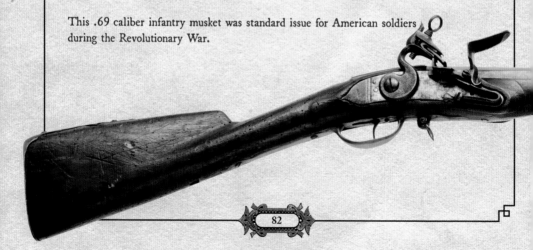

was "one of the vermin bred in [its] entrails."[13] Once outed, the so-called "Conway Cabal" crumbled. The following July 4, as the nation celebrated its second anniversary of independence, Thomas Conway was shot, but not killed, when he faced a diehard Washington supporter in a duel.

## MONMOUTH: IN THE HEAT OF BATTLE

After the defeat at Saratoga, the British guessed correctly that the French would shortly enter the war and swell opposition numbers. In response they decided to concentrate forces in New York and vacate Philadelphia.

**ABOVE:** Alexander Hamilton's oath of allegiance as Washington's aide-de-camp, dated May 12, 1778

At the end of June some fifteen hundred wagons left one city for the other. Separated by miles from the vanguard, the train's rear guard made a vulnerable target. For days, after dark and barely sleeping at all, Hamilton rode out to keep an eye on the progress of this slow-moving caravan. Returning, he briefed his commander.

On the night of June 27, upon learning that the British were encamped at Monmouth, Washington sent orders to General Charles Lee. He was to take 600 to 800 men and harass the rear guard the next morning while Washington brought up his main force to attack. Lee did so, but not with the desired result. His men traversed several ravines, were easily rebuffed, and staged a hasty retreat. Sent ahead of Washington's force to scout, Hamilton found men falling back. One of Lee's aides later reported that Hamilton "rode up in a great heat," while Lee said he was "in a sort of frenzy of valor."[14] It was not so surprising. Away from a desk and on the field at last, he was possessed by fevered exuberance.

As cannonballs and bullets took men down all around him, Hamilton's horse was shot from under him and he tumbled to the ground, his leg injured. John Laurens's mount met the same fate in the battle and so, as a matter of fact, did another combatant's— Aaron Burr. When Washington rode up and saw Lee's men fleeing, he reprimanded their commander. Rallying his troops, Washington

Lt. Col. John Laurens was critical of General Lee's performance during the Battle of Monmouth.

stayed alongside them through long hours of fighting during the blistering afternoon—"the mouth of a heated oven seemed to me but a trifle hotter," one solder recalled.[15] Hamilton asserted that Washington "took maneuvers for checking the enemy" and "directed the whole with the skill of a master workman."[16] Hours of fighting left over 350 Americans dead, wounded, or missing, with one-third of the deaths from heatstroke. British casualties were similar in number.

Two competing narratives emerged after the battle. Critics of General Lee said the unwieldy retreat of his men had prevented a much-needed American victory. Lee's "precipitate retreat spread a baneful influence every where," John Laurens wrote his father, Henry Laurens. He asserted that the whole British force "would have fallen into our hands, but for a defect of abilities or good will in the commanding officer of our

*The Battle of Monmouth* by Alonzo Chappel

advanced corps."[17] Hamilton was harsher yet, calling Lee "a driveler in the business of soldiership" and "truly childish."[18]

Lee told it differently. The enemy had gained intelligence that the Americans were about to attack and countered Lee's force handily. His men fled of their own volition, "without my orders, without my knowledge, and contrary to my inclination."[19] He had advanced as directed, and then, after his men retreated, he had held a defensive position. Washington should not have publicly admonished him in the heat of the battle. "I think, sir," he wrote two days after the battle, "I have a right to demand some reparation for the injury committed."[20]

In his stark reply Washington doubled down. He accused Lee of being "guilty of a breach of orders, and of misbehaviour before the enemy on the 28th instant, in not attacking them as you had been directed, and in making an unnecessary, disorderly, and shameful retreat."[21] To defend himself, Lee insisted on a court-martial. His wish was granted, but the tribunal found him guilty and suspended him from command for one year.

Washington leads his troops at the Battle of Monmouth.

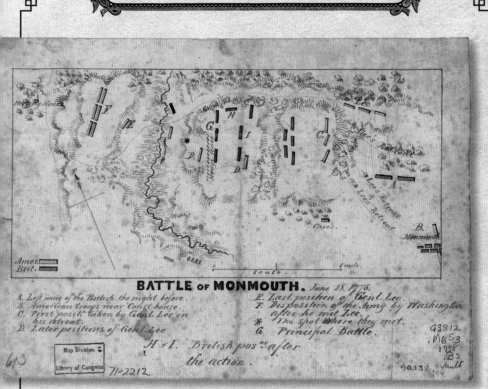

BATTLE OF MONMOUTH. June 28. 1778.

A. Left wing of the British the night before.
B. American troops near Court house.
C. First posit.n taken by Genl. Lee in his Retreat.
D. Later positions of Genl. Lee

E. Last position of Genl. Lee.
F. Disposition of the Army by Washington after he met Lee.
* The spot where they met.
G. Principal Battle.

H. & I. British pos.ns after the action.

A map showing the disposition of American and British forces at the Battle of Monmouth

Still, Lee continued to disparage Washington in letters and even in print, attacking him in December 1778 in his *Vindication to the Public*.

As commander in chief, Washington could not with dignity respond to continued assaults on his character. His devoted aides-de-camp, however, could. John Laurens challenged Lee to a duel of honor, with Hamilton his second. Lee accepted. On December 23, 1778, outside Philadelphia at "half past three" in the afternoon, Laurens and Lee "met agreeable to appointment in a wood situate near the four mile stone on the Point no point road." After Laurens shot Lee in the side, Hamilton and Evan Edwards, Lee's second, declared the duel over. The conduct of both principals, the two said, "was strongly marked with all the politeness generosity coolness and firmness, that ought to characterize a transaction of this nature."[22]

At Morristown snow fell on December 18 and remained on the ground for three months as storm after storm swept through. Extreme conditions hindered the supply lines.

# MORRISTOWN: THE HARD WINTER

In 1779 the Americans invaded pro-British Native American territories in the West, while Britain seized the offensive in the South. In the winter of that year, and into the early months of 1780, Hamilton and the Continental Army encamped in Jockey Hollow near Morristown, New Jersey. The "Hard Winter," as people called it for generations after, was the coldest recorded before or since by Euro-Americans inhabiting the Northeastern seaboard of the United States. The New York Harbor froze solid, allowing the British who controlled it to ride horses and roll cannons and haul loads of firewood between New Jersey, Manhattan, Long Island, and Staten Island. In Philadelphia, a resident complained "that the ink now freezes in my pen within five feet of the fire." Sleighs traversed the Chesapeake Bay from Baltimore to Annapolis, and salt-water inlets froze as far south as North Carolina.[23]

At Morristown snow fell on December 18 and remained on the ground for three months as storm after storm swept through. Extreme conditions hindered the supply lines. One soldier, Joseph Plumb Martin, chronicled the consequences: "We were absolutely, literally starved. I do solemnly declare that I did not put a single morsel of victuals into my mouth for four days and as many nights, except a little black birch bark which I gnawed off a stick of wood . . . I saw several of the men roast their old shoes and eat them, and I was afterwards informed by one of the officers' waiters, that some of the officers killed and ate a favorite little dog."[24]

During the winter, weather was at fault, but come spring, when rations remained scant, Martin reported that "the men were now exasperated beyond endurance. Here was the army starved and naked, and there their country sitting still and expecting the army to do notable things while fainting from sheer starvation. . . . What was to be done?"[25]

Some deserted. Others, including Martin, defied their superiors and paraded back and forth under arms. Officers who tried to interfere found "bayonets of the men pointing at their breasts." They stopped just short of mutiny, and within days a shipment of pork and thirty head of cattle arrived in camp. Months later, soldiers from Pennsylvania did mutiny, and when the New Jersey line followed suit, six were executed.

Hamilton saw all this. From Morristown he wrote of an army "without cloathing, without pay, without provision, without morals, without discipline. We begin to hate the country for its neglect of us." He noted that the problems were not natural or even military, but economic and political. The country, an unwieldy confederation of states, had barely found its legs but needed legs if it were to last longer than this war. Cognizant of the fact, Hamilton was already penning exacting, futuristic solutions. "There are epochs in human affairs," he wrote to a member of Congress, "when *novelty* even is useful."[26]

# IV

## 1780–1781

# The Power of Love

Buried in snow and swept by freezing winds as it was in 1780, Morristown did not seem to be a place where love could take fire, but it did. Marriage was on Alexander Hamilton's mind, and it was a timely next step for a man who favored durable, often impassioned attachments and who was much drawn to women.

## "I Meet You in Every Dream"

A little less than a year earlier, Hamilton had concocted an inventory of all he required in a wife. Sending it off to John Laurens, he posed in deliberately wry fashion as one world-wise man writing to another:

> She must be young, handsome (I lay most stress upon a good shape), sensible (a little learning will do),

OPPOSITE: 1787 Ralph Earle portrait of Hamilton's intensely devoted wife, Elizabeth Schuyler

well-bred . . . chaste and tender (I am an enthusiast in my notions of fidelity and fondness), of some good nature, a great deal of generosity. . . . In politics, I am indifferent what side she may be of; I think I have arguments that will easily convert her to mine. As to religion, a moderate streak will satisfy me. She must believe in god and hate a saint. But as to fortune, the larger stock of that the better. Though I run no risk of going to purgatory for my avarice, yet as money is an essential ingredient to happiness in this world—as I have not much of my own and as I am very little calculated to get more either by my address or industry—it must needs be that my wife, if I get one, bring at least a sufficiency to administer to her own extravagancies.[1]

In the middle of January Elizabeth Schuyler, the second daughter of Philip Schuyler and Catherine Van Rensselaer Schuyler, arrived. She was accompanied by her cousin from Elizabethtown, Kitty Livingston, who had flirted with young, handsome Alexander Hamilton at Liberty Hall after he first arrived in America. Now, wearing his smart uniform and holding an esteemed position under the commander in chief, he undoubtedly appeared more handsome yet. The young women stayed with Philip Schuyler's sister, Gertrude, and her husband, John Cochran, the renowned surgeon general now stationed at Morristown. Less than a half mile away was the Ford Mansion, which served as the winter quarters for George Washington and his aides-de-camp, including Alexander Hamilton. He and Eliza were soon seeking each other out in one residence or the other.

The Ford Mansion's one-time owner, Jacob Ford, had produced gunpowder in his own mill after Britain banned shipments to the restive colonies in the fall of 1774. His widow, a patriot in her own right, reserved several first-floor rooms for the use of her family and gave up the rest. At night George and Martha Washington occupied an ample sleeping chamber on the second floor while Hamilton and other aides-de-camp crowded into a smaller one. The house teemed with activity—the widow Ford's four children running about, callers coming and going on urgent missions, aides passing in and out of the large war room, and visitors appearing regularly.

"We are merry at Camp but have little to eat either for man or beast," General Nathanael Greene reported. Apparently "merry" didn't apply to the food but to dancing, which the men mentioned time and again in their correspondence. One soldier listed thirty-five officers and aides, including Hamilton, each of whom paid $400 toward the "expense which may be incurred in the promotion and support of a dancing assembly to be held in Morristown this present Winter 1780." Another, on February 1, reported the progress: "The Dancing room 70 feet long by 40 broad . . . will soon be finished in a few days, and we hope to Open the Assemblys about the middle of this month." Meanwhile, military men added new maneuvers to their training program: "There are not many able hands in the business of dancing—however they make good progress and practice very assiduously." They also assiduously sought female partners.[2]

Elizabeth Schuyler had to have been one. Much taken with her dark, lively eyes, confident demeanor, and comely figure, Alexander Hamilton sought her out. They were soon meeting daily and almost immediately fell in love. *Fell* was the operative word, with its suggestion of a sudden, irreversible descent. There was jolt on landing, but in the next instant both realized that they stood on perfectly solid ground. They determined to spend their lives together.

Alexander and Elizabeth might have married quickly, except for the example of her sister Angelica Schuyler. In 1777, when she was twenty-one, Angelica had eloped with John Barker Church, thinking her father would

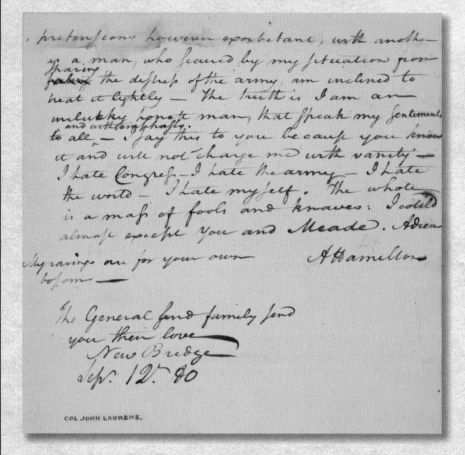

pretensions however exorbitant; with another—
a man, who seared by my situation from sharing
the distress of the army, am inclined to
heal it lightly — The truth is I am an
unlucky honest man, that speak my sentiments
to all and with too much frankness; I say this to you because you know
it and will not charge me with vanity—
I hate Congress—I hate the army — I hate
the world — I hate myself. The whole
is a mass of fools and knaves: I could
almost except You and Meade. Adieu
My ravings are for your own
bosom —                                    A Hamilton

The General and family send
you their love
New Bridge
Sep. 12. 80

COL JOHN LAURENS.

**ABOVE:** Hamilton's engagement to Elizabeth Schuyler came at a fortuitous time. The dire state of the army had cast gloom over all things political and military. In this letter to John Laurens, who had been captured in the fall of Charleston in May 1780 and was then on parole in Philadelphia, he wrote: "I hate Congress—I hate the army—I hate the world—I hate myself. The whole is a mass of fools and knaves." Yet Hamilton had found the woman of his dreams: "young, handsome, sensible, well-bred, chaste, and tender," as he had written to Laurens earlier. Elizabeth gave him hope. The letter depicted here was sent from the Zabriskie-Steuben House at New Bridge Landing in River Edge, New Jersey.
**OPPOSITE:** Major General Philip Schuyler

never consent to the marriage. In April 1780 Philip Schuyler wrote to Hamilton, "Mrs. Schuyler did not see her Eldest daughter married. That also gave me pain, and we wish not to Experience It a Second time. I shall probably be at Camp In a few days, when we will adjust all matters."[3]

With consent obtained and matters adjusted, the streetwise, all-knowing tone Hamilton had used with Laurens mutated. He wrote ardently now to Eliza or Betsey, the names interchangeable. "I have told you, and I told you truly that I love you too much. You engross my thoughts too intirely to allow me to think of any thing else—you not only employ my mind all day; but you intrude upon my sleep. I meet you in every dream—and when I wake I cannot close my eyes again for ruminating on your sweetness." He openly anticipated "those delicious caresses which love inspires and marriage sanctifies" and closed with yearning—"may you be as happy as I shall ever wish to make you!"[4]

On December 14, Alexander and Eliza were formally married at a small gathering in the Schuylers' two-and-a-half story Georgian mansion in Albany. Set on eighty acres of land and on a hill overlooking the Hudson River, its entrance hall was forty-eight feet long by twenty feet wide by twelve feet high. Wainscot shutters folded neatly against the jambs of interior windows, scenic French wallpaper adorned a wall, and decorative, elegant pillars supported a stately staircase that spiraled upwards. The inhabitants of this grand house welcomed Hamilton into the illustrious fold, no matter his origins.

The Hamilton and Schuyler wedding reception in 1780; George Washington can be seen standing at the right

Philip Schuyler saw in Hamilton a man of extraordinary intelligence, who had shown courage in battle, and who looked him directly in the eye. If he had to bet, he'd bet that he had a bright future ahead of him—Washington held him in high regard, after all. Eliza's mother nodded her approval. Eliza's three younger brothers and two younger sisters concurred. So did her older sister, Angelica, who knew something of men, having been courted and married and escorted into her husband's world three years before.

Hamilton, who had lost a family, was embraced by another. He and Philip regularly exchanged letters over the years; he teased younger sisters and surely engaged younger brothers man-to-man. The captivating Angelica would flirt for a lifetime with Hamilton, who would treat her in kind. Their correspondence speaks to a warm attachment; some wager it was more. Once Angelica wrote to Betsey and made a lighthearted proposal:, "I love him very much and if you were as generous as the Old Romans, you would lend him to me for a while."[5]

Much of the back and forth was probably nothing more than badinage and hyperbolic flourish, common in genteel eighteenth-century society. The best evidence against an affair is perhaps Eliza's unaltered allegiance to both parties and the fact that Angelica cared deeply for her, much evident in the sisters' frequent, affectionate exchange of letters. Besides, if Eliza had lent Hamilton out for long, he might not have been the elder sister's best choice. He was a workhorse who rarely took a reprieve. His mind raced with ideas, and his quill travelled at the same approximate speed when he put thought to paper.

Hamilton would never have taken Angelica off to Paris, as Church did. She resided for two years there and for a dozen years more in London, where her mate served in Parliament. In ornate drawing rooms and ballrooms, she magnetized illustrious men with her wit and bearing and sparkling intelligence. Church enabled his wife's ambitions. Owing in part to his position, she ascended to a social pinnacle. She chose a mate who also filled a reigning criterion that Hamilton embraced—"But as to fortune, the larger stock of that the better," as Hamilton had told Laurens. Church made that fortune supplying both the French and American armies during the Revolutionary War.

For his part, Hamilton had initially asked for a wife who was sensible, chaste, tender, faithful, fond, good-natured, and generous. He chose well in selecting Eliza.

# A PARTING

Two months following his marriage, on February 16, 1781, Hamilton quarreled with Washington. Shortly afterward, he detailed what had happened, writing to his father-in-law. In a draft of his lengthy letter Hamilton crossed out dozens upon dozens of words and phrases and added others. Obviously he labored, and obviously he knew that Philip Schuyler admired Washington and that his own leave-taking risked offending him.

"I am no longer a member of the General's family," he opened. Washington had called for him, but rather than coming "immediately," he delivered an urgent letter to another aide and then conversed for "about a minute" with Lafayette. Afterward he stood before Washington:

> "Instead of finding the General, as is usual, in his room,
> I met him at the head of the stairs, where accosting me in
> an angry tone, 'Colonel Hamilton,' said he, 'you have kept
> me waiting at the head of the stairs these ten minutes. I
> must tell you, Sir, you treat me with disrespect.'"

Accused, Hamilton instinctively fired back, as a man conscious of honor might: "I replied without petulancy, but with decision, 'I am not conscious of it, Sir; but since you have thought it necessary to tell me so, we part.' 'Very well Sir (said he), if that be your choice.'"[6]

The seemingly instantaneous exchange was more than that. It emerged during war, when the pressures were unremitting. Quarters were

General Washington and his staff. Hamilton had tired of his subordinate status.
"I always disliked the office of an Aide de Camp as having in it a kind of personal
dependence"

crowded, rations short, nights sleepless, conferences long, tasks never-ending, and critics omnipresent. There were also underlying tensions. Hamilton was restless, hoping to fight in the war; Washington was weary, hoping the war would soon end. More than once Hamilton had asked for a field command, but Washington repeatedly denied him. Most of all, Hamilton had tired of his subordinate status. "I always disliked the office of an Aide de Camp as having in it a kind of personal dependence," he told Schuyler. Subservience, for the prideful Hamilton, fostered resentment. "For three years past I have felt no friendship for him and have professed none. I wished to stand rather upon a footing of military confidence than of private attachment."

Less than an hour after the blow-up, Washington sent a message to Hamilton. The incident "could not have happened but in a moment of passion." He was willing to forget it. Hamilton was not, but he did assure Schuyler that his leave-taking would not disrupt Washington's affairs. "I did not wish to distress him or the public business, by quitting him before he could derive other assistance by the return of some of the gentlemen who were absent."[7]

The rupture was perhaps inevitable, but it was not permanent. Years later, when nation-making, not war, was at issue, Washington would have need of Hamilton and Hamilton of Washington. They shared a vision for a strong and united country and to realize it, each man depended on the other.

## LOVE TESTED: YORKTOWN

In the north, when Hamilton left Washington, the war seemed to be at a standstill. Some seven months earlier, in July 1780, nearly 6,000 French soldiers dispatched by King Louis XVI and under the command of the

Comte de Rochambeau landed in Rhode Island. This mighty force did not, however, do much to immediately advance the revolutionary cause. The British effectively blockaded the French fleet in Narragansett Bay, hemming them in. For their part, the Americans were incapable of dislodging the British from their strongholds in Rhode Island and New York. Whenever the king's army attempted to advance inland, on the other hand, Continental forces repelled their attacks, aided by local militia. Neither side weighed in with a culminating, decisive victory.

Intent on breaking the stalemate in the North, the British had shifted their focus and launched an aggressive campaign in the South. In 1778 they captured Savannah. In May 1780, after a six-week siege at Charleston, they fired heated shells that set buildings ablaze in a grand finale that forced the city's surrender. They now controlled two critical harbors on the sea. Lord Charles Cornwallis, the British commander, then turned inland, expecting to find backcountry loyalists who were roused by these victories and who would now flock to his side. What he discovered instead was a sharply divided population, both loyalists and their antagonists. The two sides collided in ferocious battles.

Cornwallis achieved tactical victories, but his men were repeatedly tested and guerilla bands attacked his supply lines. The cost of the conquest was unsustainable and in the end he retired to the coast. By the spring of 1781, Cornwallis was in Virginia facing troops under the command of the Marquis de Lafayette. Outnumbered, Lafayette harassed Cornwallis's men but would not confront them head-on. "Was I to fight a battle," he wrote to Washington in May, "I'd be cut to pieces, the militia dispersed, and the arms lost. I am therefore determined to skirmish, but not to engage too far."[8] He wrote Hamilton, detailing the numbers: "We have 900 Continentals; their Infantry is near five to one; their Cavalry ten to one; our Militia are not numerous, come without arms, and are not used to war."[9]

Comte de Grasse, the commander of the French fleet

In the summer Washington moved his camp to Dobbs Ferry on the Hudson River. Desperate for field service, Hamilton travelled there; he intended to make his case for the last time. Forcing the issue, he enclosed his commission in the letter he submitted to his commander. If Washington did not act at once, he would serve in no capacity at all. Not wanting to lose Hamilton altogether, Washington assured him of a field command. Immediately Alexander wrote Eliza, "Though I know my Betsy would be happy to hear I had rejected this proposal, it is a pleasure my reputation would not permit me to afford her. I consented to retain my commission and accept my command."[10] She would not be happy but, as his wife and as the daughter of a military man, she realized that there were no sidelines in a war, not for the men who marched or the women they left. War tested everyone.

Now in charge of an advance battalion of New York infantry, Hamilton began in a business-like way to order up tents, camp kettles, pails, shoes, stationery, and other necessities. When the shoes were denied him, he went straight to the top. Washington complied; Hamilton's men would have the shoes.[11]

As Hamilton readied for action, the commander in chief weighed options for a new campaign. New York's loss still rankled him, and it was close at hand, a tempting target, but incoming intelligence pointed in another direction, toward the South. Cornwallis had received orders from above. He was to locate a defensible deepwater port in Chesapeake Bay that could be readily supplied and serve as a base for the British naval fleet. Before long he made his choice—Yorktown, set on a peninsula and surrounded on three sides by the Chesapeake Bay waters.

Meanwhile, the Comte de Grasse, the commander of a French fleet, sent word that he had left the French West Indies and was sailing toward the Chesapeake Bay. All heralded the news—his presence could make all the difference. What made Yorktown particularly vulnerable was the narrow neck through which any oceangoing vessel had to pass when approaching or departing the city. The French armada could, like a cork in a jug, stop up the opening and prevent the British from delivering aid and also hamper any attempt on Cornwallis's part to escape by sea. Suddenly Yorktown seemed ikely prey. If the operation succeeded, the rewards would be immense.

Washington made his decision and sent off orders. The Marquis de Lafayette was to pin Cornwallis in place on the ground and await De Grasse. When De Grasse arrived, these two could set the trap, and after the Franco-American military materialized, the combined forces would spring it.

Hamilton's battalion was in a marching line of French and Continental soldiers who passed cheering crowds in Philadelphia and continued southward. In five weeks' time they were at the York River. By late September some 17,000 American and French soldiers were positioned at Yorktown, more than double the British numbers. Parties of light infantrymen and riflemen reconnoitered enemy positions while others skirmished with pickets of British soldiers. Exacting regulations were issued to enforce order among the disparate units of enlisted men.

When the British abandoned several outer positions, retiring closer to Yorktown, allied troops immediately occupied the territory and erected redoubts, the small, temporary forts that afforded protection in the field. Working nonstop, they moved howitzers and other siege pieces closer, fashioned sandbags, and transported stores. On a cloudy night, under a lightly falling rain, and under the direction of engineers, fatigue parties began to dig out a trench that would bring them closer and closer to York-town. Maintaining a strict silence, soldiers shoveled out the sandy soil and tossed it high to fashion sheltering embankments. It wasn't until first light that the British realized what had happened and that they were now vulnerable. Sheltered inside an existing trench, the enemy could readily extend the line.

By the ninth of October, artillery companies came within range of the town, and the incessant, deafening bombardment began. Shells and cannonballs careened through the air day and night. On the eleventh returning fire exploded over the diggers all night as they worked to construct a second parallel trench that approached the town. By morning only two British redoubts stood in the way of final victory, numbers nine and ten, which had to be taken. An attack was ordered for the night of October 14.

That morning, Hamilton drilled his light company in full sight of the enemy. One soldier, Ephraim Slattery, expected British fire and was dumb-founded when it didn't erupt. "I can think of no other reason that they don't kill us all except maybe they're too astonished," he testified.[12] Hamilton wanted to astonish. He had been held back overlong, chafing at the constraint. In the thick of it at last, unleashed, he was close to maniacal. But he proved his valor at the expense of the men he exposed. There was no purpose in it, no adversary to defeat or field position to claim. Later that night, however, there was an adversary and a position and reason for valor.

OPPOSITE: This map detail of Yorktown shows British lines and disposition of American and French forces.

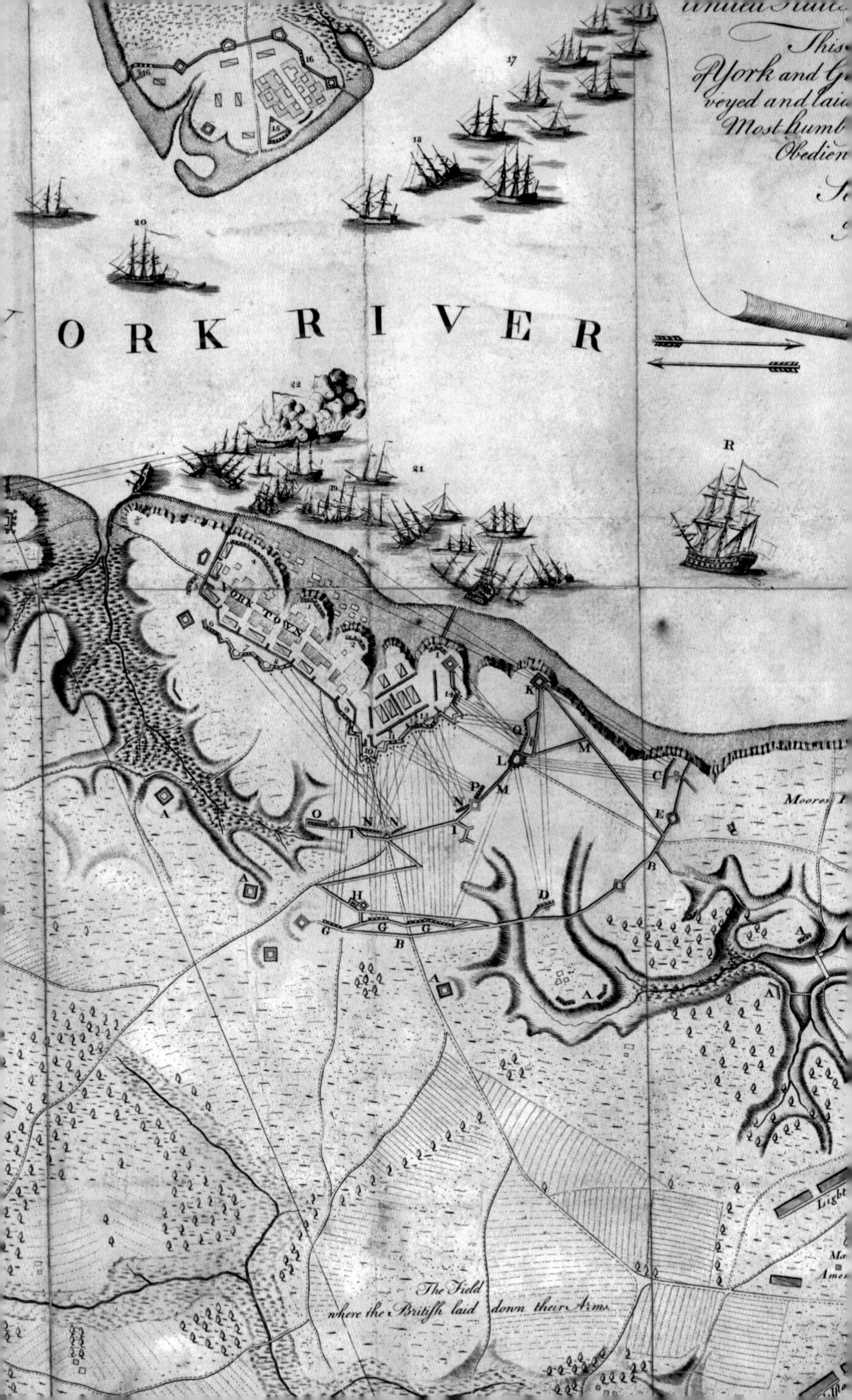

United States

This
of York and G
veyed and laid
Most Humb
Obedien

Se
9

YORK RIVER

16

17

18

20

42

21

19

21

R

YORK TOWN

K

Q

M

L

C

M

E

P

M

N

B

A

O

N

N

Moores P

H

D

A

G

G

B

A

A

A

A

Light

M
Amer

The Field
where the British laid down their Arms

ABOVE: French painter Eugene-Louis Lami's *Storming a Redoubt at Yorktown* (1840) illustrates the dramatic assault by French and American soldiers on two British redoubts. OPPOSITE: This British officer's "small sword" is believed to have been surrendered by Cornwallis after the battle of Yorktown.

After dark, a French corps of 400 chasseurs and grenadiers charged Redoubt Nine. Within Lafayette's American Light Infantry, Hamilton led a corps of men, four hundred strong, who were to take Redoubt Ten; John Laurens, with men from his battalion, was in those ranks. As if Hamilton had personally designed a spectacular entry, the three comrades allied. Hamilton's company stormed Redoubt Ten so rapidly that they overtook the sappers who generally stripped a redoubt of the sharp stakes and tree limbs protecting it. Within ten minutes it was all over. In his report, in a flat understatement, Hamilton said that "the ardor of the troops was indulged," as was his.[13]

With obstructions removed, the artillery incessantly battered a town that was now only four hundred yards off. On the night of October 16, in a desperate attempt at evacuation, a fleet of small boats set onto the York River, but a sudden, howling storm sent them helter-skelter in all directions. They struggled back to shore. The next morning a redcoated boy appeared on the Yorktown parapet, beating his drum. The officer at his side waved a white handkerchief.

Two days later Cornwallis surrendered but pleaded illness and did not personally present his sword to the victors. His ground troops and seamen, 8,000 combatants altogether, marched between two cordons. The French line formed up on one side "in complete uniform" and "displayed a martial and noble appearance," an eye witness recorded. On the other side were the Americans, who, "though not all in uniform nor their dress so neat, yet exhibited an erect soldierly air."[14]

On that same day Hamilton wrote his new wife. Pride ran beneath the surface of the confession he made. "Two nights ago, my Eliza, my duty and my honor obliged me to take a step in which your happiness was too much risked. I commanded an attack upon one of the enemy's redoubt; we carried it in an instant, and with little loss. You will see the particulars in the Philadelphia papers." He then assured her, "There will be, certainly, nothing more of this kind."[15]

Yet the war was not quite done. It would take more than a year to negotiate a preliminary treaty. In the interim irregular

warfare surfaced, and not until September 3, 1783, was the Treaty of Paris signed. Some ten months after Yorktown, on August 15, 1782, Alexander Hamilton wrote a letter to John Laurens, whose company was entangled in conflicts that still erupted near British-held Charleston. It was sent from Albany, where Hamilton was not only safe but on the verge of joining the Continental Congress as a delegate:

"Peace made, My Dear friend, a new scene opens. The object then will be to make our independence a blessing. To do this we must secure our union on solid foundations;

PRECEDING: John Trumbull's *Surrender of Lord Cornwallis* (1820) is displayed in the U.S. Capitol's rotunda. BELOW: Benjamin West's *Treaty of Paris* (c. 1783) shows (L–R) John Jay, John Adams, Benjamin Franklin, Henry Laurens, and William Temple Franklin; the British delegation would have been painted at right but they refused to pose. OPPOSITE: The final page of the Treaty of Paris, signed September 3, 1783

without Difficulty and without requiring any Compensation.

## Article 10th.

The solemn Ratifications of the present Treaty expedited in good & due Form shall be exchanged between the contracting Parties in the Space of Six Months or sooner if possible to be computed from the Day of the Signature of the present Treaty. In Witness whereof we the undersigned their Ministers Plenipotentiary have in their Name and in Virtue of our Full Powers signed with our Hands the present Definitive Treaty, and caused the Seals of our Arms to be affix'd thereto.

DONE at Paris, this third Day of September, In the Year of our Lord one thousand seven hundred & eighty three. —

D Hartley    John Adams.    B Franklin    John Jay

*The Death of Colonel John Laurens* by Howard Pyle (1899)

a Herculean task and to effect which mountains of prejudice must be leveled! Quit your sword my friend, put on
the toga, come to Congress. We know each others sentiments, our views are the same; we have fought side by
side to make America free, let us hand in hand struggle to
make her happy."[16]

It is doubtful that Laurens read the missive. On August 27, when
he set out with troops to attack a British foraging party near Charleston,
dozens of soldiers ambushed the detachment. Instead of charging away
from heavy musket fire, he charged toward it and was killed.

Earlier, in March 1780, Hamilton had sent another letter. This one
Laurens certainly did read:

"Adieu my Dear; I am sure you will exert yourself to save your country; but do not unnecessarily risk one of its most valuable sons. Take as much care of yourself as you ought for the public sake and for the sake of yr. affectionate A. Hamilton

All the lads remember you as a friend and a brother. Meade says God bless you."[7]

Hamilton and Laurens shared a reckless courage and much else, but only one would wear a toga. The other would not be there for the "public sake."

# V

# *Model Citizen*

HAMILTON LEFT YORKTOWN AND WAR BEHIND AND MADE HIS WAY TO Albany, where Eliza was in her eighth month of pregnancy. Arriving ill, he was in and out of bed for weeks, his life on hold. For six years he had lived a military life, its regimens and structures sharply delineated. Now he stood on the other side of the war's wide and bloody divide. In the civilian world there were no assigned duties and no chain of command. He would take charge of his life.

## ALEXANDER HAMILTON, MEET AARON BURR

To support his growing family, Hamilton decided to resume his legal studies. The law was a gateway to a possibly lucrative career and provided

**OPPOSITE:** Trumbull's 1806 portrait of Hamilton

access to the political sphere. Since newly enacted punitive legislation barred Tory attorneys from entering the courtroom, the field was ripe for the picking. While a three-year apprenticeship had previously been required of a newly graduated legal scholar, veterans were now fast-tracked if they had, like Hamilton, studied jurisprudence before their military service. He could enter the courtroom after passing a bar exam. This exception was the work of another aspiring law student, Aaron Burr, who had also interrupted his studies to join the war effort. Burr's petition for favorable treatment for the country's heroic men-at-arms had won favor with the New York legislature.

Like Hamilton, Burr pursued his law studies in Albany. In October 1781, just weeks before Hamilton would arrive, Burr showed up at Philip Schuyler's grand residence with a letter of introduction: "This will be handed to you by Lieutenant Col. Burr, who goes to Albany, to solicit a license in our courts."[1] Schuyler invited Burr to use his well-stocked library, and when Hamilton arrived and commenced his studies, the two shared that resource. Their lives intersected at this point; the record clearly shows it.[2]

The two ambitious, astute, and striking young men were enough alike that a long and amicable friendship seemed possible and even probable. They were of medium height and held themselves erect, soldier-like. Hamilton was Burr's senior by only a single year. Misfortune visited both men during their childhoods: Burr was orphaned early, his father dying in 1757 when he was a toddler and his mother dying the next year. After taking Burr and his sister in, his maternal grandparents died within a year

OPPOSITE: Aaron Burr. ABOVE: Charles Willson Peale's watercolor portrait of Hamilton (c. 1780)

Major General Israel Putnam, c. 1775. Burr, after serving as aide-to-camp to
Washington, later attached himself to Putnam.

as well. Even though tragedies piled on early, Burr's place in the world, unlike Hamilton's, was auspicious and durable. He was descended from a long line of high-ranking reverends, one the distinguished Calvinist Jonathan Edwards, who preached that but for the grace of God man was eternally damned. For Burr, opportunity was a given, not a dogged quest as it was for Hamilton. Still, when Burr was thirteen and the youngest in his College of New Jersey class, he didn't rely on status to get by. Instead he toiled away at his studies for sixteen to eighteen hours a day, his pace never slacking, a Hamiltonian trait.

Once launched into the world, the men led roughly parallel lives. At times one seemed to brush against the other without noticing, like a pedestrian hurriedly passing another headed in the same direction. Both entered the Revolutionary War at its commencement. Both fled to Harlem Heights when the British landed a savage force at Kips Bay. Some historians say Burr led the way, rescuing Hamilton; others ignore or deny that account. Burr was praised for the part he played at the beginning of the war in the expedition to Quebec, while Hamilton, late in the game, proved himself at Yorktown. On the field at Monmouth, Hamilton's horse was shot out from under him while the murderous heat felled Burr. But did they speak that day or note one another? Who can know?

Both were aides-de-camp to Washington, Burr briefly, before attaching himself to General Israel Putnam. During the war, as aides and officers and combatants, they rubbed shoulders with men who would play key roles in nation-building. They travelled widely, gaining perspective, and, in Hamilton's case, a distaste for state parochialism. Having signed up for revolution when barely out of their teens, they were seasoned men of the world as it drew to a close.

Seeing them side-by-side up close, an observer would note Burr's dark hair, hazel eyes with large, black pupils, and his warm coloring.

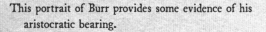

This portrait of Burr provides some evidence of his aristocratic bearing.

Hamilton's brown hair had a fiery, auburn cast and his skin was light, flushed at the cheeks. Burr might regard another gentleman steadily, holding him in a cold, piercing gaze, as if he could see through to his bones. Hamilton, roused by whatever he himself was saying, would study a companion eagerly, awaiting a response. If Burr turned his head to the side, an aristocratic profile came into view, the high forehead and nose joining in a perfectly smooth slope of bone. Hamilton's nose jutted out like that of a combatant, its line uneven and the profile craggy. If there were similarities, there was also stark contrast.

## FOR LOVE OF PUBLIC CREDIT

Aaron Burr and Alexander Hamilton aspired to a political life, but while no overarching goal steered Burr, a singular issue captivated Hamilton—public credit, and, in turn, the fragility of an economic system that hobbled along without it. His interest wasn't abstract. He had lived alongside men who, in a winter's war, marched through snow without shoes or gnawed on bark because the commissary did not have the wherewithal to supply them.

A systems man at heart, Hamilton saw beyond the commissary's ineptitude. It lacked funds because under the Articles of Confederation, Congress could not levy taxes but only ask for monies from states that didn't always come through. Shortchanged, Congress borrowed from

French or Dutch creditors, who might cut off funds if loans weren't paid. It also issued paper money, which soon lost the lion's share of its value because in fact it had very little—nothing backed it. By 1780 a dollar could not purchase a penny's worth of goods. Without underpinnings, the rickety economic structure quavered and then collapsed.

As early as 1780, when Hamilton was still Washington's aide-de-camp, he complained to a congressman that the body "meddled too much with details of every sort."[3] It should, he proposed, place its business affairs in the hands of a single person. In his presumptuous way, Hamilton suggested Robert Morris, who had made a fortune through profiteering in the French and Indian War and was perhaps the nation's most prosperous merchant. Five months later, when Congress created an executive post of superintendent of finance, Morris was in fact asked to fill it.

Immediately upon hearing of Morris's appointment, Hamilton sent off a letter of congratulations. After the obligatory civilities, he just happened to mention that he had urged Congress to create the position and had then put forward Morris's name. He then assured Morris of his allegiance by summarizing their shared stance: "'Tis by introducing order into our finances—by restoreing public credit—not by gaining battles, that we are finally to gain our object." Finally came the pitch: "I take the liberty to submit to you some ideas, relative to the object of your department."[4] What followed, penned by a young man with no official credentials in economics, was a lengthy treatise on the public finances of European nations and calculations for the adaptation of those systems in the United States. The centerpiece of Hamilton's plan was a monopolistic national bank.

Most of the tome he sent off was in Eliza's writing, marked by her characteristic misspellings.[5] Alexander must have talked to her of his ideas, and she must have believed in them if she wanted, literally, to have a hand in the venture. One can imagine him watching her as she wrote, head bent, industrious in his cause. From the start the marriage was a warm collaboration.

Morris had already envisioned a national bank, and upon assuming office he officially proposed one. Only nine days later, on May 26, 1781, Congress chartered the Bank of North America, empowered to issue bills of credit that would function as currency. Then, placing himself at considerable risk, the man people called "The Financier" issued "Morris Notes," drafts of $20 to $100, redeemable in specie, signed by himself and watermarked "United States." He vowed that if the government couldn't make good on these notes, he would. "My personal credit, which thank Heaven I have preserved throughout all the tempests of the War, has been substituted for that which the country had lost."[6] It was a unique and courageous act.

Morris's fix was only temporary. Not unless states played their part and paid into the national treasury, as Congress perpetually begged them to do, could the seriously indebted nation become solvent. Morris pressed the nation's case, and he hired the young Hamilton to figure out what New York should contribute and then collect that amount. It wasn't easy to play the intermediary between the Financier and New York's legislature, but when Hamilton presented that body with the bill it owed to the nation, legislators were so impressed that they asked him to represent their state in Congress.

Once there, the rising star crunched numbers as few others could— but those in the revenue column were never enough, representing, as they did, whatever the thirteen states reluctantly forked over. Unless Congress actually raised funds of its own, solvency was out of the question. At Morris's urging, Congress proposed a 5 percent impost on imported goods to pay off wartime debts. Twelve states approved, but Rhode Island, which levied its own state impost on imported goods, refused. Under the Articles of Confederation, the young nation's working constitution, any alterations

**ABOVE:** Robert Morris. **FOLLOWING:** George Washington wishes his Continental Army officers goodbye at the end of the Revolution in 1783.

required unanimous approval. A single state could kill a measure a dozen others wanted—and did in this instance.

Unable to place the nation's finances on a permanent footing, Robert Morris finally resigned. Hamilton too retired from the Office of Finance, and he also left Congress after serving just a single session. In the third week of July 1783, Hamilton wrote Eliza, telling her, "I give you joy, my angel." He was about to return and promised that they would soon be "happily settled in New York."[7]

# New York City: Two Lawyers Settle In

Many one-time New Yorkers were now returning to the city, but it was not the same as when they left. During the seven years of British occupation, buildings had been gutted and used for barracks, hospitals, or stables. Military men had installed themselves in private residences that owners deserted, and returning owners found shattered furniture and general mayhem. Along the streets, stately trees had been felled for firewood. Refuse was scattered everywhere. Two fires, the Great Fire in September 1776 and another in early August 1778, had destroyed some eight hundred houses, leaving ghostly brick skeletons or sheer rubble in their wake.

Tories who had settled in New York now fled in droves, and more would depart by Evacuation Day, officially designated as November 15, 1783. Hamilton worried that even "second class" merchants "may carry away eight or ten thousand guineas. . . . Our state will feel for twenty years at least the effect of the popular frenzy."[8] As usual, while others angrily fumed, he pulled out his tally sheet and calculated the cost. If he worried about the adverse financial effect, he also worried about an outright miscarriage of justice as "popular frenzy" took hold. Here was mob spirit, blind as ever and always Hamilton's bugaboo.

Late in 1783 Alexander and Elizabeth Hamilton rented a Manhattan house at 57 Wall Street, in a genteel, relatively unscarred neighborhood with brick homes set back from cobblestoned streets. Nearby were shops and a general bustle. Their son Philip, born almost two years earlier— when Hamilton told the Marquis de Lafayette that he was "rocking the cradle"—would spend his childhood in this house.[9] Hamilton's legal work provided an adequate income for his budding family. He took on a broad

**ABOVE:** John Joseph Holland's *A View of Broad Street, Wall Street, and the City Hall* (1797). **FOLLOWING:** A map illustrating the damage caused in New York by the Great Fire of 1776

array of cases, mostly civil but some criminal. His fees were modest, and at times he worked pro bono, never amassing substantial savings and purposely avoiding, as he did in public life, any sign of financial impropriety.

Aaron Burr and the woman he had married the previous year also moved to Wall Street, but to the east of the Hamiltons at 3 Wall Street, which was in a better neighborhood. Theodosia Burr was ten years' Burr's senior and formerly the wife of Jacques Marcus Prevost, a British officer she had married when she was seventeen and who died of battle wounds in Jamaica. After being overcome by heat prostration at Monmouth, Burr

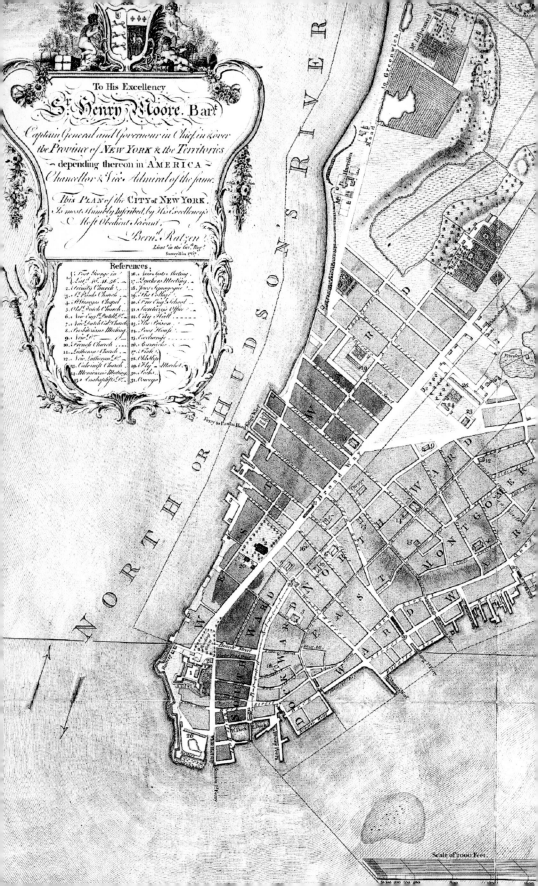

To His Excellency
S.ʳ Henry Moore. Bar.ᵗ
Captain General and Governour in Chief in & over
the Province of NEW YORK & the Territories
depending thereon in AMERICA
Chancellor & Vice Admiral of the same.
This PLAN of the CITY of NEW YORK.
Is most Humbly Inscribed, by His Excellency's
Most Obedient Servant
Bern.ᵈ Ratzen
Lieut.ᵗ in the 60.ᵗ Reg.ᵗ
Surveyed in 1767.

## References:

1. Fort George in
   Lat. 40. 42. 58.
2. Trinity Church
3. S.ᵗ Pauls Church
4. S.ᵗ Georges Chapel
5. Old Dutch Church
6. New Eng.ᵈ Dutch D.ᵒ
7. New Dutch Cal.ᵗ Church
8. Presbiterians Meeting
9. New D.ᵒ
10. French Church
11. Lutheran Church
12. New Lutheran D.ᵒ
13. Calvinist Church
14. Moravians Meeting
15. Anabaptists D.ᵒ

16. Seceders Meeting
17. Quakers Meeting
18. Jews Synagogue
19. The Colledge
20. Free Charity School
21. Sec:retarys Office
22. City Hall
23. The Prison
24. Poor House
25. Exchange
26. Barracks
27. Fish
28. Old Slip
29. Fly — Market
30. Docks
31. Oswego

NORTH OR HUDSON'S RIVER

Scale of 2000 Feet.

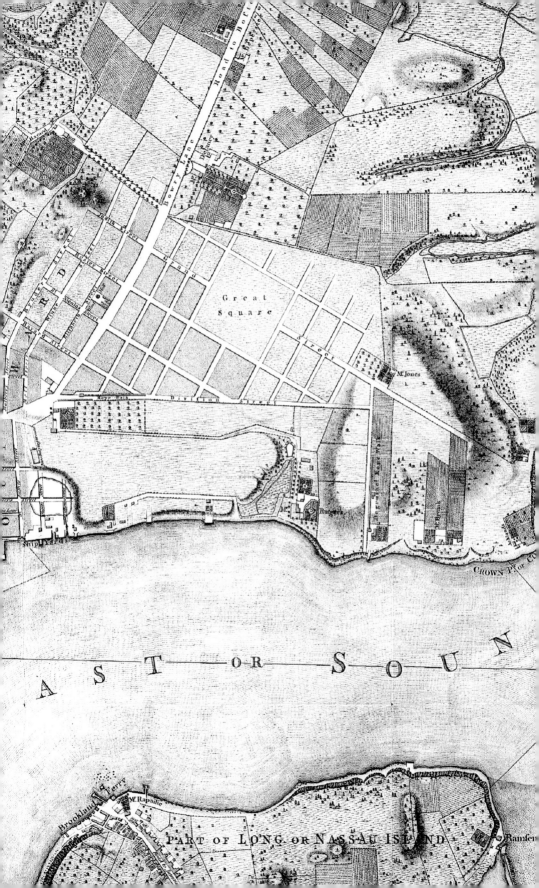

had recovered at the Hermitage, the Prevost's ninety-three-acre estate, where he and Theodosia formed an attachment.

On the face of it Theodosia was an unlikely choice for a man who reputedly toyed with women. She was no toy—in her reading repertoire were the four volumes of Edward Gibbon's *History of the Decline and Fall of the Roman Empire* and other erudite works. Burr wasn't put off by her erudition, as most men in the age might have been, but enthralled. Together he and Theodosia poured over Mary Wollstonecraft's radically feminist *Vindication of the Rights of Woman*. In addition to her intelligence, Theodosia was also generous, a devoted mother to five children and a welcoming, capable hostess to both British and American officers. She was brave enough to battle for possession of the Hermitage and had to because in point of law the estate belonged to a British officer. As such, it was subject to confiscation. Burr valued these qualities in Theodosia. Long after she died, he would be entirely devoted to the daughter she bore in this year, 1783. At his insistence, she was named Theodosia after her mother.

When the Burrs dined at the Hamiltons' or the Hamiltons at the Burrs', Theodosia and Elizabeth entertained in proper style, and Aaron and Alexander conversed with civility. In court they might find themselves on opposite sides, but they also shared cases as colleagues. There was harmony.

## PLAYING BY THE RULES

Hamilton specialized in the defense of former Loyalists whose estates were being confiscated, believing they should have their day in court. When the New York legislature passed punitive laws against them, he issued two highly charged pamphlets. True patriotism, he said, was "generous, humane, beneficent and just" and was not evidenced by self-professed patriots who had argued for the legislature's "arbitrary act." They only wished to "inculcate revenge, enmity, persecution, and perfidy" by playing on "all the furious and dark passions of the human mind." What galled him most was that the measures confiscated property and punished people "without regular trial and conviction."[10] They weren't playing by the rules and that was sure to anger Hamilton.

Meanwhile other rules, rules he abided by, declared that enslaved humans were property. The state of New York had more slaves than any other in the North. At one time Philip Schuyler owned up to twenty-seven slaves who worked his mills and fields and the household of his estate.[11] Historians debate whether or not Alexander and Eliza Hamilton ever claimed ownership of others, but all agree that Alexander helped the Schuyler clan, especially Angelica and John Church, obtain slaves. Perhaps he trusted that they would treat their slaves fairly or excused the purchase simply because of its legality. In any case the seizure of their property without their consent wasn't an option.

Hamilton addressing three judges with others looking on in courtroom

On the flip side, Hamilton believed men could change the rules and take down the institution of slavery. He was not alone. Many believed that while slavery was unlikely to be abolished instantaneously, it could be gradually done away with. In the interim, he and other well-meaning New Yorkers tried to convince individuals to manumit, or free, their slaves.

In 1785 Hamilton and like-minded advocates formed the New-York Society for Promoting the Manumission of Slaves, and Protecting Such of Them as Have Been, or May be Liberated. Over half the society's members, including its chairman, John Jay, and member Aaron Burr, owned slaves but were open to freeing them if they could ensure their livelihood and prevent their being captured and re-enslaved. Hamilton and his close friend Robert Troup served on the three-man committee that addressed apprehensions like these and developed an orderly, voluntary set of rules for members.[12]

As a public-minded citizen, Hamilton busied himself in a myriad of projects that promoted education. In his mind, institutions of learning served as springboards to advancement and leveled the playing field. There too he created workable systems. He served on the New York State Board of Regents, which in 1784 reopened King's College, his alma mater, and renamed it Columbia College. Teaming up with John Jay, he wrote Columbia's charter, which is still operative today. To prepare students for college, he helped create Erasmus Hall Academy, today's Erasmus Hall High School, the state's first chartered secondary school.

No cause was too small to attract Hamilton's attention. He pushed to remove a disfigured statue of William Pitt from Wall Street and to raise the roadbed in the middle so it could properly drain. But no cause was too large either, and nothing intrigued Hamilton more than banks.

Beyond the prospect for personal gain, banks systemized credit and the flow of money. The Bank of North America helped stabilize currency, but it alone could not facilitate the concentration of capital and economic

# A

# DIALOGUE

### CONCERNING THE

# SLAVERY

## OF THE

# AFRICANS;

Shewing it to be the *Duty* and *Interest* of the *American*
States to emancipate all their *African* Slaves.

## WITH AN

## ADDRESS to the owners of such SLAVES,

## DEDICATED TO THE HONOURABLE THE

# CONTINENTAL CONGRESS.

To which is prefixed, the Institution of the Society, in
NEW-YORK, *for promoting the Manumission of Slaves,
and protecting such of them as have been, or may be,
liberated.*

Open thy mouth, judge righteously, and plead the cause
of the poor and needy.        PROV. xxxi. 9.
And as ye would that men should do to you, do ye also to
them likewise.        LUKE vi. 31.

NORWICH: Printed by JUDAH P. SPOONER, 1776.

# NEW-YORK:

Re-printed for ROBERT HODGE.

M,DCC,LXXXV.

This 1776 pamphlet promoting the emancipation of slaves was reprinted by the
New York Manumission Society in 1785.

development in every locale. That would take regional banks. In 1784 Hamilton and a group of investors petitioned the state legislature to charter the Bank of New York. When it balked, Hamilton and company established the bank as a purely private venture, with no ties to the state. Henceforth, people could park money at the bank, saving it, while those needing funds for investments could borrow at steady, reliable interest.

Banks also need rules, and Hamilton wrote this bank's constitution. There would be thirteen directors, chosen in a manner that blended democracy with plutocracy: "That every Holder of one or more Shares to the Number of Four, shall have One Vote for each Share—A Subscriber of Six Shares shall have Five Votes, Eight Shares, Six Votes, and Ten Shares, Seven Votes, and One Vote for every Five Shares above Ten."[13]

Wise to the ways of the world, Hamilton instituted safeguards against corporate takeovers. Shareholders with stock purchased within

Hamilton reading from his constitution for the Bank of New York, which he founded in 1784

three months of an election could not vote, and out-of-state shareholders could not assign proxies to vote in their name.

The bank flourished. Shares were bought and sold on the open market, and when the New York Stock Exchange opened in 1792, Bank of New York shares were among the first traded. "Wall Street" was born, with Hamilton, who resided at 57 Wall Street, a midwife. The infant bank, growing through mergers and acquisitions, later became a corporate giant, the Bank of New York Mellon Corporation.

## STATE OR NATION?

After retiring from Congress in 1783, Hamilton departed the public arena. He had, however, assumed the political assets and liabilities of the Schuylers and the Van Rensselaers through marriage, and New York politics commanded his attention. Before the Revolution, these and other ruling clans, some owning upwards of one hundred thousand acres, dominated New York's politics. Then came the war, and with it George Clinton.

Clinton was born to Scotch-Irish immigrants, not landed gentry. After service in the French and Indian War, this parvenu studied law and in 1768 ran for, and won, a seat in the New York Provincial Assembly, representing rural Ulster County. Once there he resisted British imperial policies at every turn. Known as a war hawk, when war actually broke out, Clinton was commissioned a brigadier general. After the Declaration of Independence turned colonies into states, New York's revolutionary new constitution decreed that the people would choose the governor, a duty allocated elsewhere to state legislatures. Newly empowered, the electorate chose one of their own, George Clinton.

Henceforth, New York's great manorial families such as the Schuylers had to compete with Clinton for political power. Hamilton quickly sized up his coming opponent: "He is, I believe, a man of integrity and passes with his particular friends for a statesman, [but] his passions are much warmer, than his judgment is enlightened." He panders, Hamilton asserted, to "prevailing prejudice, . . . especially when a new election approaches."[14] Hamilton was not an adherent of "prevailing prejudices," but they played in Clinton's favor. He stayed in office for twenty-four years. During Clinton's tenure, as Hamilton ascended to power, the two clashed repeatedly. Hamilton valued banks; Clinton suspected them. Clinton hounded Loyalists; Hamilton defended them. In Hamilton's view, Clinton was, above all, "a man of narrow and perverse politics," always "opposed to national principles."[15] Clinton in turn weighed in, accusing Hamilton of being "very anxious to effect that ruinous measure, a *consolidation of the states.*"[16]

The existing rules favored Clinton. The Articles of Confederation allowed for no more than a confederation of sovereign states. There was no central government as we now know it. Congress could not pass laws, levy taxes, or enforce its will, so it had no way of intruding on Clinton's domain. New York even raised its own funds by levying an impost on goods imported through its harbor, including ones headed toward neighboring New Jersey or Connecticut. Financial self-sufficiency worked well for New York but not for the United States. In 1783, for the second time, Congress proposed a federal impost on imported goods. As they had in 1781, twelve states approved, but one did not, this time New York. With Governor Clinton in the lead, New York's interests trumped the country's.

Hamilton, of course, took Congress's side. To the depths of his soul, he was pro-tax—he never met a tax he didn't like. Years later, when drafting a farewell address that President Washington would give to the nation, he explained why: "Cherish public Credit as a very important source of

OPPOSITE: First page of the Articles of Confederation, drafted in 1777 and ratified in 1781

# To all to whom

these Presents shall come, we the under signed Delegates of the States
affixed to our Names send greeting. Whereas the Delegates of the
United States of America in Congress assembled did on the fifteenth day
of November in the Year of our Lord One Thousand Seven Hundred and
Seventy seven, and in the Second Year of the Independence of America
agree to certain articles of Confederation and perpetual Union between the
States of Newhampshire, Massachusetts bay, Rhodeisland and Providence
Plantations, Connecticut, New York, New Jersey, Pennsylvania, Delaware,
Maryland, Virginia, North Carolina, South Carolina and Georgia
in the Words following, viz. Articles of Confederation and perpetual
Union between the states of Newhampshire, Massachusetts bay, Rhodeisland
and Providence Plantations, Connecticut, New York, New Jersey, Pennsylvania, Delaware, Maryland, Virginia, North Carolina, South Carolina
and Georgia.

**Article I.** The Stile of this confederacy shall be "The
United States of America."

**Article II.** Each state retains its sovereignty, freedom and
independence, and every Power, Jurisdiction and right, which is not by
this confederation expressly delegated to the United States, in Congress
assembled.

**Article III.** The said states hereby severally enter into a firm
league of friendship with each other, for their common defence, the security
of their Liberties, and their mutual and general welfare, binding themselves to assist each other, against all force offered to, or attacks made upon
them, or any of them, on account of religion, sovereignty, trade, or any other
pretence whatever.

**Article IV.** The better to secure and perpetuate mutual friendship
and intercourse among the people of the different states in this union, the
free inhabitants of each of these states, paupers, vagabonds and fugitives
from Justice excepted, shall be entitled to all privileges and immunities of
free citizens in the several states; and the people of each state shall have
free ingress and regress to and from any other state, and shall enjoy therein
all the privileges of trade and commerce, subject to the same duties, impo-
sitions and restrictions as the inhabitants thereof respectively, provided
that such restriction shall not extend so far as to prevent the removal of
property imported into any state, to any other state of which the Owner
is an inhabitant; provided also that no imposition, duties or restrictions
shall be laid by any state, on the property of the united states or either of
them.

    If any Person guilty of, or charged with treason, felony, or
other high misdemeanor in any state, shall flee from Justice, and be found
in any of the united states, he shall upon demand of the Governor or
executive power, of the state from which he fled, be delivered up and removed to the state having jurisdiction of his offence.

    Full faith and
credit shall be given in each of these states to the records, acts and judicial
proceedings of the courts and magistrates of every other state.

**Article V.** For the more convenient management of the general
interests of the united states, delegates shall be annually appointed in such
manner as the Legislature of each state shall direct, to meet in Congress
on the first Monday in November, in every year, with a power reserved
to each state, to recal its delegates, or any of them, at any time within the
year, and to send others in their stead, for the remainder of the Year.

strength and security. . . . Recollect that towards the payment of debts there must be Revenue, that to have revenue there must be taxes, that it is impossible to devise taxes which are not more or less inconvenient and unpleasant. . . . A spirit of acquiescence in the measures for obtaining revenue which the public exigencies dictate is in an especial manner the duty and interest of the citizens of every State."[17] Taxes were an inconvenient truth in the 1780s. During the war, Americans had been taxed to death, and they were currently caught in a sweeping recession. Merchants demanded specie, or coins—not notes of credit. Customers simply didn't have hard cash and fell into debt. Once in debt, they couldn't pay taxes to the states, and when Congress asked the states for money, the states had little to give. In 1785 the states came through with only 20 percent of the money Congress requisitioned.

The infant nation was in free fall, held hostage, in Hamilton's view, by "narrow" men like Governor Clinton who opposed "national principles." Other Americans blamed creditors and tax collectors and asked a disturbing question—was this the price of freedom?

"War is indeed a rude, rough nurse to infant states," said Gouverneur Morris, who had worked with Hamilton under Robert Morris. Peace was "not much in the interest of America," he contended, for it made people less willing to tolerate a strong, central government that could place the nation on a firm financial footing.[18] The nation had survived the war, but could it survive the peace?

OPPOSITE: Ezra Ames' portrait of Governor George Clinton (1804)

# VI

## 1786–1787

# Envisioning a Nation

HAMILTON CHERISHED ORDER AND DEPLORED THE NATION'S economic and political dysfunction. This was not how things were supposed to work.

## BRIGHT IDEAS

So how *should* things work? At King's College Hamilton rummaged through works by Bacon, Hume, Locke, and Montesquieu in search of answers. During his army days he carried the six volumes of *Plutarch's Lives* and two volumes of *The Universal Dictionary of Trade and Commerce* everywhere he went. These texts were his workman's toolkit and as familiar to him as a hammer in a carpenter's hand. By the age of twenty-five, having immersed himself in the history and philosophy of

OPPOSITE: This Trumbull portrait of Hamilton with the Bank of New York's constitution was commissioned in 1791 by New York merchants who wanted to express their gratitude to Hamilton for "the Important Services you have rendered Your Country"

state-building, he in effect felt he could build one. When James Duane, a delegate from New York to the Continental Congress, turned to Hamilton for advice on how to cure the nation's ills, Washington's young aide-de-camp penned an authoritative 7,051-word response. Although not "the sober views of a politician," as he conceded, it detailed his "ideas of the defects of our present system, and the changes necessary to save us from ruin."[1]

Inefficiency had no place in the government he envisaged. In part inefficiency grew out of "an excess of the spirit of liberty which has made the particular states show a jealousy of all power not in their own hands." (Ironically, Hamilton wrote this from a place called Liberty Pole, near Morristown.) While that spirit had propelled the revolution, it paralyzed governance.

"Nothing appears more evident to me, than that we run much greater risk of having a weak and disunited federal government, than one which will be able to usurp upon the rights of the people," Hamilton proclaimed. Unless remedies surfaced quickly, he suspected the new nation might simply fall apart. In an empire like Britain's, "the danger is that the sovereign will have too much power," but in a confederation of states, the danger is a lack of power "sufficient to unite the different members together, and direct the common forces to the interest and happiness of the whole." To prove his point, the self-taught scholar marshaled evidence from the ancient Grecian republics, the Swiss cantons, the Germanic states, and the United Provinces of the Netherlands, all of which failed, or were failing, for lack of cohesion.

Hamilton went on to spell out the various components of a new government, what job each component would perform, and how they

OPPOSITE: James Duane, a New York delegate to the Continental Congress who turned to Hamilton for advice on alleviating the financial crisis

would function together. Economic control was paramount. Whoever "holds the purse strings absolutely, must rule," he wrote. The new plan of government, first and foremost, "should provide certain perpetual revenues, productive and easy of collection, a land tax, poll tax or the like, which together with the duties on trade and [the sale of] the unlocated lands would give Congress a substantial existence, and a stable foundation for their schemes of finance." These would be taxes *with* representation—but taxes nonetheless and no more begging from the states.

Beyond taxation, Hamilton proposed vesting the federal government with a score of equally crucial powers. They ranged from "all that relates to war, peace, trade, finance, and to the management of foreign affairs" to "coining money" and "establishing banks." Excepting the last, the solutions he contrived at the age of twenty-five were written into the United States Constitution seven years later.

## National and Supreme

Committed nationalists like Hamilton were a distinct minority in the early post-war years. As a delegate to Congress in 1783, Hamilton drafted a resolution that detailed the problems with the Articles of Confederation and called for a national convention to amend them. The "public safety" was threatened, he observed, by the "annihilation of public credit." If the nation were invaded, nobody would lend it money to put up a defense because Congress had no way to pay back its debts. Only by granting Congress "the *power of general taxation*" could the nation stand on its own accord. His point was well taken, but he never even presented his plan. On the draft he wrote: "Resolution intended to be submitted to Congress at Princeton in 1783; but abandoned for want of support." The ailing nation was not yet ready to receive his remedies.[2]

After quiting Congress, Hamilton watched its finances spiral downward for the next three years, but in 1786, by his own account, "the derangement of our public affairs, by the feebleness of the general confederation, drew me again reluctantly into public life."[3] In that year he won a seat in the New York Assembly. His short-term objective was to get that body, which had blocked the 5 percent federal impost, to reverse itsposition. His long-term goal was to reconfigure, and strengthen, the federal government. He would fail in the first but succeed in the second.

Just as Hamilton reengaged with politics, the Virginia legislature called for a national convention to meet in Annapolis, Maryland, in September. Its job was straightforward—to frame federal regulations of trade. Ever the political strategist, and something of a wolf in sheep's clothing, Hamilton imagined the convention as "a stepping stone to a general convention, to form a general constitution," soon to be known, of course, as the Constitutional Convention.[4] He lobbied the New York legislature to send delegates to Annapolis; he was, he indicated, available.

The legislature chose Hamilton and five others as delegates, but only two went: Hamilton and Egbert Benson, who also yearned for a strong central government. In those days, Hamilton did not often leave Eliza alone with Philip (age four), Angelica (not yet two), and Alexander, Jr., (only three months old), but business called—the business of the nation, that is. On September 1, the day he left, he apologized to a friend for not dining with him: "Mrs. Hamilton insists on my dining with her to day as this is the day of departure and you (who are not a prophane batchelor like Benson) will know that in such a case implicit obedience on my part is proper."[5]

At Annapolis ten other delegates from four states joined the New York emissaries. It was hardly an impressive showing but it was a blessing in disguise. All men "were unanimously of opinion, that some more radical reform was necessary," Hamilton wrote.[6] Without dissent, the Annapolis Convention called upon all states to appoint delegates to a larger convention that would "devise such further provisions as shall appear to them necessary to render the constitution of the Federal Government adequate to the exigencies of the Union." That convention, the one Hamilton envisioned, was to meet in Philadelphia the following May.

The Philadelphia convention might have fared no better than Annapolis, save for the raucous events that fall and winter. In that time the "exigencies of the Union" grew steadily more apparent. Indebted farmers, under arms, closed courts throughout Massachusetts. The governor called out the militia, but half the militiamen sided with the rebels. Debtors also closed courts in South Carolina, Virginia, Maryland, and New Jersey. In Pennsylvania farmers prevented tax collectors from seizing their cattle. The Rhode Island legislature, under the sway of debtors, issued paper money, and New York, North Carolina, and Georgia were considering the same recourse. With the value of money plummeting, neither Congress nor the states could find willing lenders, and public credit was at risk.

Congress was powerless. There was no federal army to speak of, only a few hundred soldiers in western forts. Congress was also penniless. From October 1786 through March 1787 the states paid a grand total of $663 into the federal treasury. To use a modern idiom, the government was so small that it was drowning in the bathtub. Hamilton had predicted that fate and all now seemed to sense the danger.

This was the nationalists' political moment. Practically no one had come to Annapolis, but all states except Rhode Island sent delegates to the

OPPOSITE: This 1850 reprint of a famous early Philadelphia map illustrates the young city's roads, canals, and important landowners. This is the first known sketch of the Philadelphia State House, later Independence Hall, where the Constitutional Congress met.

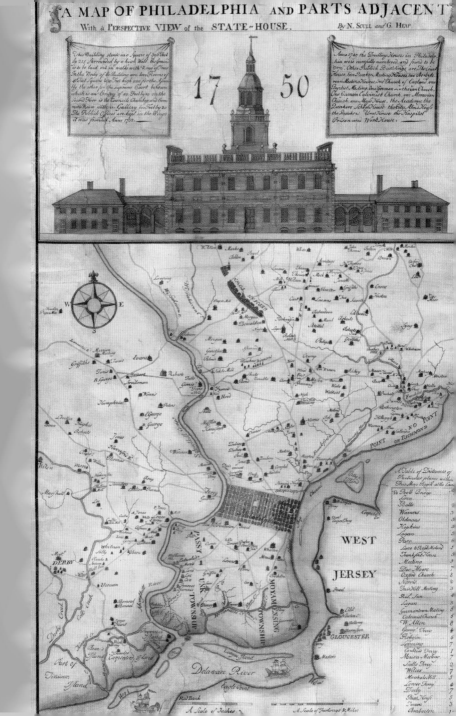

Annapolis in the State of
Maryland Sept 11th 1786 —

At a Convention of Commissioners appointed by sundry States, in consequence
of a recommendatory Resolution of
the Legislatures of the State of
Virginia, for the purpose "of taking
" into Consideration the Trade of the
" United States to examine the relative
" Situation and Trade of the said States
" to consider how far an uniform
" System in their commercial
" Regulation may be necessary
" to their common Interest and their
" permanent Harmony, and to report
" to the several States such an Act
" as, when unanimously ratified by
" them, will enable the United States
" in Congress assembled to effectually
" to provide for the same"

Present
Alexander Hamilton } New York
Egbert Benson —

Abraham Clarke
William C. Houston } New Jersey
James Schureman

Tench Coxe — Pennsylvania

John Dickinson
George Read } Delaware
Richard Bassett —

Edmund Randolph
James Madison — } Virginia
Saint George Tucker

Mr Dickinson was unanimously
elected Chairman

The Credentials produced by the
Commissioners from the respective
States were read and from the
Credentials produced by the New York
and New Jersey Commissioners from the
State of New York and the Commissioners
from the State of Pennsylvania
it appeared that three Commissioners

so-called "federal convention" in Philadelphia. Even George Washington emerged from his retirement to attend and, eventually, preside. He wrote to Thomas Jefferson, the nation's minister to France at the time: "That something is necessary, all will agree; for the situation of the General Government (if it can be called a government) is shaken to its foundation and liable to be overset by every blast.—In a word, it is at an end, and unless a remedy is soon applied, anarchy and confusion will inevitably ensue."[7]

By May 14, 1787, the appointed day, only delegates from Pennsylvania and Virginia were in Philadelphia. In this age, when travel was difficult and uncertain, tardiness was common. A fallen tree might block a road or rough weather slow a carriage. Hamilton arrived on the eighteenth, and not until May 25 did the Convention finally achieve a quorum of seven states. On that day, twenty-nine men gathered in the Assembly Room of the Pennsylvania State House and took their seats in Windsor chairs before writing tables, arranged in an arc around the presiding officer's platform. The space was not overlarge, and someone who spoke in a conversational tone could be heard by another. For the better part of four months, delegates remained in this room from eleven to four thirty daily, excepting Sundays. In Philadelphia's muggy heat, the quarters felt oppressive at times, and there was no opening the high windows to let in air because delegates wanted to ensure that no one standing outside could hear what transpired within. It was essential that the delegates say exactly what they thought, and that everything be said.

No dirt farmers could be found here, although there were plenty of gentleman planters. Also present were merchants and a healthy share of graduates from Princeton, Yale, and Harvard, the nation's preeminent

OPPOSITE: Minutes of the proceedings of the 1786 Annapolis Convention, where Hamilton called for the Articles of Confederation to be amended

| Abraham Yates | John Lansing Jr. | Gouverneur Morris |

colleges. Well over half of the delegates, like Hamilton, practiced law—
a fitting occupation for the task at hand.

On that very first day, to nobody's surprise, George Washington was
unanimously chosen to preside. He spoke only once on an issue, and that
on the very last day. More emblem than participant, he provided a sense
of gravitas and propriety. If the Convention seemed to exceed its commission, he tilted the whole bumptious affair toward legitimacy.

New York had dispatched Hamilton, Robert Yates, and John Lansing
Jr. At the outset Hamilton found himself in a bind. In setting its procedural
rules, the Convention determined that each state, not each delegate, had a
single vote. As subalterns in Governor Clinton's camp, Yates and Lansing
opposed the centralization of authority, and the two outvoted Hamilton
at every turn. Voting, however, was only one way to participate. Hamilton
could still offer motions, present plans, and serve on committees. Most of
all he could speak his mind freely, which he certainly did.

The New York legislature issued binding instructions to its delegates, as
did all the states. It sent Hamilton, Yates, and Lansing to Philadelphia "for
the sole and express purpose of revising the Articles of Confederation."[8]
That was one constraint. There was another. Under the Articles of

Confederation, a ruling did not take effect unless "confirmed by the several States," and *several* meant *all*. New York, or any single state legislature, could eventually kill the Convention's recommendations by refusing to ratify them. The system empowered naysayers, not innovators. It is said that the perfect is the enemy of the good. But when configuring rules to govern a nation, unanimity was the enemy of solutions or remedies.

At the Convention Hamilton and several other delegates at once took that naysaying bull by the horns. In dramatic fashion, they challenged a mild opening resolution: "The Articles of Confederation ought to be . . . corrected and enlarged." Not strong enough, the nationalists said. Virginia's Edmund Randolph and Gouverneur Morris, who now represented Pennsylvania, moved to delete those words and substitute in their stead: "A *national* government ought to be established consisting of a *supreme* legislative, executive & judiciary." (James Madison's meticulous notes on the Convention emphasized the words "national" and "supreme.") This motion set off a spirited discussion "on the force and extent of the particular terms *national & supreme.*" Some delegates noted that they were only authorized by their state legislatures to amend the Articles of Confederation, not to abolish them, but Gouverneur Morris countered, "In all communities, there must be one supreme power, and one only." A confederation was no more than "a mere compact resting on the good faith of the parties," he explained, while a "national, supreme" government implied "a compleat and compulsive operation."

Of the eight states present, six voted to create a new national government with supreme authority over the constituent states. Hamilton, of course, voted in favor of this revolutionary transformation, but within New York's delegation, his "aye" was cancelled out by Yates's "nay." (Lansing had not yet arrived.)

## "Solid Plan Without Regard to Temporary Opinion"

Hamilton was well versed in constitution-making. He had recently drafted constitutions for Columbia College and the Bank of New York as well as a strategic plan for New York's Manumission Society. Years earlier, he had detailed a plan for economic recovery and outlined what a truly national government might look like. He was more than ready for the task at hand.

Yet for three weeks, as others debated the construction of the legislative and executive branches in a new government, Hamilton held his tongue and held fire. Finally, shortly after eleven on a Monday morning, June 18, he rose from his seat and took the floor. For the rest of the day, uninterrupted by any other speaker, he delivered what was undoubtedly the most memorable speech of the summer.

Hamilton stated point-blank that the United States government should be based on the British model. A hereditary monarch, he said, possessed so much power, privilege, and influence that he craved no more and was therefore above corruption. He understood that America would never accept a king or a queen and talked instead of a "governor" who bore a strong resemblance. Although this monarch-like potentate was to be elected, he would serve for life. Removed from popular influence, he could keep a tight grip on the reins of the government and prevent disruption.

Senators would also serve for life. Once in a generation, as senators or the governor died off, people would have some say in choosing new ones. Technically, because the "offices are open to all men," this qualified as a republican government—but barely so. "We ought to go as far in order to attain stability and permanency as republican principles will admit," he declared in his speech. The notes he jotted down in preparation for the

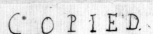

C O P I E D.

1 — Objection to the present confederation

I Entrusts the great interests of the nation to hands
  incapable of managing them —

    Treaties of all kind
    All matters in which foreigners are concerned —

    The care of the public peace : Debt

    Power of treaty without power of execution


    Common defense without power to raise troops
    have a fleet — raise money


    Power to contract debts without the power
    to pay —


    — These great interests of the state must be
    well managed or the public prosperity
    must be the victim —

  Legislates upon communities,
  Where the legislatures are to act they
  will deliberate —                    ⌠ To ask money not to co ___
                                       ⌡ & by after unjust measures —
  No sanction —                          Legal

989

Hamilton's notes for a speech proposing a plan of government at the Federal Convention
in June 1787

speech went further: "It is said a republican government does not admit a vigorous execution. It is therefore bad; for the goodness of a government consists in a vigorous execution."

State governments, said Hamilton, were "not necessary for any of the great purposes of commerce, revenue, or agriculture." They might be useful as "subordinate Jurisdictions," but certainly not sovereign entities. If they "were extinguished," he argued, "great œconomy might be obtained."

Hamilton asserted that he was not advocating a return to monarchy and abolition of the states, even though those were his preferences. That would "shock public Opinion too much." He was also aware that his plan "went beyond the ideas" of most delegates. But if they had the courage to lead, the people might follow. "The people will in time be unshackled from their prejudices; and whenever that happens, they will . . . be ready to go as far at least as he proposes."[9]

Stunned and fatigued, no delegate spoke after Hamilton concluded his marathon discourse. The Convention adjourned for the day, and when delegates reconvened the next morning, they took no account at all of what Hamilton had said. Not until three days later was there even a mention. Then, William Samuel Johnson of Connecticut made a passing reference to Hamilton's "boldness and decision," adding that although "he has been praised by every body, he has been supported by none."[10]

If delegates refused to entertain his ideas, why the praise? Whether friend of foe, all were awed by his intellect and his sheer stamina. Hamilton never ceased to amaze. A delegate from Georgia by the name of William Pierce was in the habit of creating thumbnail sketches of delegates and in sketching Hamilton he remarked on his depth.

> Colo. Hamilton is deservedly celebrated for his talents.
> . . . he enquires into every part of his subject with the

searchings of phylosophy, and when he comes forward he comes highly charged with interesting matter, there is no skimming over the surface of a subject with him, he must sink to the bottom to see what foundation it rests on. His language is not always equal, sometimes didactic, . . . at others light and tripping. . . . He is about 33 years old, of small stature, and lean."

Hamilton himself had served on the committee of three that established a rule pledging delegates to secrecy. Only because of it could Hamilton put forth what he characterized in his notes as a "solid *plan* without regard to temporary *opinion*."[12] Murmurings about his speech still leaked out, and forever after, rumors of what he supposedly said behind closed doors fueled his political enemies. Some of the rumors were true.

## HAMILTON SIGNS ON

Days after his speech, ignored if not rebuffed, Hamilton abandoned the steamy assembly chamber in the Pennsylvania State House and headed north. From New York, he reported to Washington that people he encountered on his way home actually favored the prospect of an "energetic" government. "No motley or feeble measure can answer the end,"[13] he pronounced.

Washington agreed. "The crisis is equally important and alarming," he wrote. "I almost despair of seeing a favourable issue to the proceedings of the convention." Washington laid the blame on "narrow minded politicians" who pushed "local views" at the expense of a strong and united government. The general and his aide were allies still: "I am sorry you went away. I wish you were back."[14]

Weeks later, Hamilton returned briefly to the Convention. On August 13 he championed the cause of immigrants like himself. When

Howard Chandler Christy's depiction of the Constitutional Convention, commissioned for the 150th anniversary of the signing of the Constitution and completed in 1940

Elbridge Gerry suggested that eligibility for the House of Representatives "be confined to Natives," Hamilton objected. "The advantage of encouraging foreigners" was obvious, and they would be more tempted to come if treated "on a level with the first Citizens."[15] (In the end, the Convention required representatives to be "seven Years a Citizen of the United States.")

Then, still displeased with "the Scheme of Govt. in General" that was on the table, he left again. He wanted to give the new government a "higher tone." Yet despite his dissatisfaction, he would not abandon the Convention. On August 28 he asked Rufus King of Massachusetts to tell him "when there was a prospect of your finishing as I intended to be with you, for certain reasons, before the conclusion."[16]

What were those "certain reasons"?

We can only guess, but we know that when Hamilton returned on September 6, he threw himself into the thick of the action. The proposed new government was "better than nothing," he announced, and "as he meant to support the plan," he would help fine-tune it. Days later, despite his spotty attendance, the Convention appointed Hamilton to the five-man Committee of Style, charged with preparing a final draft. Delegates might not embrace his ideas, but they certainly appreciated his "Style."

On September 17, 1787, the final day of the Convention, Hamilton gave his qualified endorsement. Although "no man's ideas were more remote from the plan than his were known to be," the choice "between anarchy and Convulsion on one side, and the chance of good to be expected from the plan on the other" was obvious. With George Washington, James Madison, Benjamin Franklin, and thirty-five other delegates, Alexander Hamilton affixed his name to the proposed Constitution.[17]

So ended the first act, but there was another act to follow. The framers declared that the new Constitution would not take effect until ratified by special conventions, chosen by the people, in nine of the thirteen states.

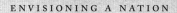

Constitution signature page

This was revolutionary in two respects. First, the process bypassed state legislatures, which stood to lose power under the new arrangement. The Constitution was to be a contract between "We, the People" and their new national government. Second, upon no authority but their own, the framers made it impossible for naysayers in a single state, whether New York or Rhode Island or any other, to thwart their plan. Whereas thirteen states could never agree to form "a more perfect union," nine states just might.

# VII

## 1787–1788

# Power of the Pen

THE FEDERAL CONVENTION (WHAT WE NOW CALL THE CONSTITUTIONAL Convention) was still in session, and the *Pennsylvania Gazette* was optimistic: "The Year 1776 is celebrated for a revolution in favor of *Liberty*. The year 1787, it is expected, will be celebrated with equal joy, for a revolution in favor of *Government*."[1] But the people who joyfully celebrated *Liberty* had suffered under the British regime's authoritative control and were wary of *Government*. Would they approve the framers' handiwork?

## BECOMING PUBLIUS

Not even all of the framers approved. On September 12, just days before the Convention adjourned, Virginia's George Mason attempted to add a declaration of rights. Not one state delegation supported his motion.

OPPOSITE: Trumbull portrait of Hamilton, c. 1792

Immediately, on the back of his printed copy of the Committee of Style's draft, he scribbled objections to the plan, and he then refused to sign the document. As soon as the Convention was over, he distributed a list of his dozen objections far and wide, garnering support for opposition.

At stake were the ground rules for a fledgling nation; contention was ubiquitous, understandably so. It surfaced in the nation's budding press, which nourished any quarrel, much as blogs, tweets, talk radio, and cable news do today. Thousands of letters and essays appeared, some favoring the Constitution, others denigrating it either entirely or in part.

At times New York squabbles and national ones intermingled. When the Convention's work was still underway, the state's Governor Clinton openly opposed the Constitution. Hamilton immediately called him out in a public letter, claiming that Clinton had a "greater attachment to his *own* power than to the *public good*."[2] Clinton supporters instinctively fired back at Hamilton. In late September, as he was resuming his New York City life, a vicious satirical piece popped up, the nation's first version of a birther myth. Under the pseudonym "Inspector," its author imagined Hamilton as "Tom S**t," who was a "mustee" (a person with one-eighth African ancestry)—and Washington as his "immaculate daddy." The caricature continued: "I have also known an upstart attorney, palm himself upon a great and good man" in order to become "known and respected." He "was at length found to be a superficial, self-conceited coxcomb, and was of course turned off, and disregarded by his patron."[3] Every reader understood the reference to Hamilton and Washington, as, naturally, Hamilton did. Incensed, he asked Washington to deny the slanderous allegation. Washington did—Hamilton had not asked to join Washington's family but was "envited thereto," and he had quit by his "own choice."[4]

Hamilton engaged in verbal fisticuffs like this when cornered, but he preferred to face able combatants on much higher ground. The time was ripe. Essays on ratification emerged in newspapers regularly, the arguments cogent on both sides. Even so, they were scattershot. Never willing to settle for less when there could be more, Hamilton imagined an extended defense of the proposed Constitution that progressed methodically and persuasively, clause by clause. He had a very specific audience in mind, the New York voters who would soon choose delegates to the state's ratification convention.

Early in October, Hamilton boarded a sloop headed up the Hudson River with its cargo and two dozen passengers. It would take him to Albany, where he had business before the state supreme court. Eliza and Alexander took the journey often enough, and she would later recall that it "usually occupied a week" and that "public business so filled up his time that he was compelled to do much of his studying and writing while traveling" on the vessel. Away from the city's hubbub and the political gossip that cluttered a mind, he could take stock of his ideas. Winds filled the vessel's sails, nudging it gently northward. The fresh air was a relief after the onslaught of smells from slaughterhouses, rendering plants, manure, and refuse. His mind cleansed, new thoughts entered. Hamilton jotted them down. It was on that sloop, Eliza reminisced, that "my beloved husband wrote the outline of his papers in *The Federalist*."[5] Days later, on the return voyage, Hamilton composed the first of eighty-five essays now known as *The Federalist Papers*. He planned to publish the essays individually in newspapers and subsequently as a single-volume collection, where its various parts would fit neatly together.

It was an ambitious venture from the first, and more so before long. The following year Archibald McLean, whom Hamilton engaged to print the book, wrote: "When I engaged to do the work, it was to consist of twenty Numbers, or at the utmost twenty-five, which I agreed to print for thirty pounds." To McLean, that seemed like a manageable number; he could print 500 copies of the combined essays, to be sold for six shillings. But the project soon took on a life of its own. "The Work increased from 25 numbers to 85," McLean wrote, and for the same price he had to deliver two large volumes instead of a single smaller one.[6]

Facing a tight deadline, Hamilton sought help from collaborators. His first choice was fellow New Yorker John Jay, a longtime political ally who had befriended the young immigrant in the prewar years. Hamilton described Jay as "a man of profound sagacity & pure integrity," and that he was.[7] A superb writer and legal scholar, Jay had coauthored New York's Constitution, served as the state's chief justice, helped negotiate the 1783 Treaty of Paris, and was currently Congress's secretary of foreign affairs. Most significantly, he agreed with Hamilton on the need for a strong central government and was among the most influential foes of Governor Clinton. Jay signed on and quickly penned four essays, but he then fell ill and remained incapacitated for several months.

Hamilton turned next to Gouverneur Morris. Born into New York's gentry, Morris was a master wordsmith and the chief author of the Constitution's final draft. But Morris was more eager to focus on his private business interests and turned Hamilton down.

Hamilton then approached James Madison, who was, in William Pierce's telling, "a gentleman of great modesty,—with a remarkable sweet temper . . . easy and unreserved among his acquaintances." Hamilton, in contrast, was "engaging in his eloquence" with "ornaments of fancy," his manners "tinctured with stiffness, and sometimes with a degree of vanity

OPPOSITE: John Jay, the first Chief Justice of the United States from 1789 to 1795, was the first American statesman of international reputation whom Gilbert Stuart ever painted. The success of this likeness of the chief justice, painted in New York in 1794, introduced Stuart to an appreciative clientele in America.

that is highly disagreeable."[8] Although not as extreme as Hamilton, Madison shared his preference for federal over state powers. Just before the Convention, he told Washington it was "absolutely necessary" that the national government possess "a negative *in all cases whatsoever* [his emphasis] on the legislative acts of the States, as heretofore exercised by the Kingly prerogative.[9]

Madison was in New York as a delegate to Congress. Fortuitously, that body had disbanded after its meeting on October 27, unable to muster a quorum for the remainder of the year. That left Madison with time on his hands and he agreed to partner on the project.

Following the custom of the time, Hamilton, Jay, and Madison wrote anonymously, with all three adopting the same pseudonym. Writers on both sides of the ratification debates liked to fashion themselves as Roman statesmen—Agrippa, Brutus, Caesar, Cato, Cincinnatus, and so on. Hamilton, the organizer of the project, chose Publius, a pseudonym he had first used in 1778. There were several famous Romans by that name, but Hamilton likely meant Publius Valerius Publicola, a founder of the Roman Republic featured in his well-thumbed *Plutarch's Lives*. At least one historian, however, conjectures that the name might refer to Publius Syrus, who was captured and enslaved during the Roman conquest of Syria.[10] His talented theatrical improvisations and his witticisms won him his freedom and great renown. Perhaps it's a stretch but might Alexander Hamilton, of lowly origins and from a foreign land, have claimed Publius as a kindred spirit?

## THE FEDERALIST

Hamilton took the lead, penning the first *Federalist* essay and publishing it in New York's *Independent Journal*. Right from the start, without

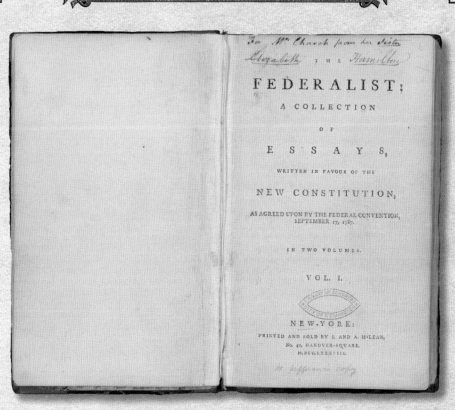

Original title page of *The Federalist*, published in 1788; the essays were not published as *The Federalist Papers* until 1961.

apology, he announced that Publius would be offering "arguments" to convince readers that "the safest course for your liberty, your dignity, and your happiness" was to adopt the new plan of government. "Yes, my countrymen, I own to you that, after having given it an attentive consideration, I am clearly of opinion it is your interest to adopt it," he wrote. "I will not amuse you with an appearance of deliberation when I have decided. I frankly acknowledge to you my convictions, and I will freely lay before you the reasons on which they are founded."[11]

Hamilton and Jay wrote at a rapid, sometimes breakneck, pace. During the Christmas season of 1787, Hamilton published six essays in a nine-day period; Madison topped that in January, putting out seven essays in nine days. Jay would write only one more essay, in March. Altogether, Hamilton wrote fifty-one essays, Madison twenty-six, Jay five, and Hamilton and Madison collaborated on three. Although there was some overlap, Madison wrote mostly about the legislative branch and federal–state relations; Hamilton covered matters of commerce, taxation, defense, and the executive and judicial branches; and Jay addressed foreign relations under the new form of government.

"Publius" addressed all his letters "To the People of the State of New-York," a far different audience than the framers at the Constitutional Convention. There, Hamilton and Madison were among like-minded gentry, mostly of a nationalist bent. Now, they faced citizens of all ranks whose primary allegiance was to their own state; most had never travelled to any other. The Constitution established federal supremacy over those states. That alone could be a nonstarter but it also vested executive authority in a single person, gave Congress an almost unlimited power to levy taxes, and created a standing army. If people were to vote in favor of concepts like these, they needed persuading.

A lawyer by trade, Hamilton knew how to argue the case he was given and set to it. While at the Convention, in his daring speech on June 18, he admitted that his ideas were not "the sober views of a politician," but he now became one. The "public Opinion" he once had dismissed was his primary concern, and time and time again, in order to win the public over, he made an abrupt about-face. At the Convention he had proclaimed "that the British Government was the best in the world, and that he doubted much whether any thing short of it would do in America." In particular, he said the president "ought to be hereditary, and to have so much power, that it will not be his interest to risk much to acquire more." Now he boasted there was a "total dissimilitude" between the American president and the "King of Great-Britain, who is an hereditary monarch." Then,

he had wanted to give the chief executive an absolute "*negative* upon all laws about to be passed"; now, he contended that in the new Constitution "the qualified negative of the president differs widely from this absolute negative of the British sovereign." Then, he had revealed a deep disregard for republican ideals; now, he assured readers that their president would be a true republican.[12]

Such reversals, in today's terms, are called "flip-flops." The phrase vilifies individuals who do not hold to perpetually fixed views, but if views are shaped by circumstances, perhaps they ought to change when circumstances do. Certainly Hamilton believed that and believed in a corollary notion—politicians were there to fix what needed fixing. Even if the constitutional contract was not of his making, it was desperately needed and he prayed that the nation's citizens would concur.

Publius mustered convincing arguments but, when all was said and done, did not convince many people. Although his work circulated among the Federalist elite, few in the general public even read the essays. More than one thousand commentaries, whether favoring or opposing ratification, appeared in the newspapers of the day. Many, after publication in a local paper, were reprinted in other cities and states. Of these, some 250 authored by other polemicists appeared in newspapers in six or more states, but only one of Publius's did, the first.[13]

By contrast, James Wilson's speech in support of the Constitution went viral. Originally delivered at the State House Yard in Philadelphia, it was reprinted in twelve of the thirteen states and in thirty-four newspapers and in twenty-seven different towns, ranging from Portsmouth to Augusta.[14] Yet after *Federalist* No. 16, only one of the sixty-nine additional Publius essays crossed New York's borders even once; in Exeter, New Hampshire, the *Freeman's Oracle* picked it up.[15] These numbers suggest that Publius was among the *least* read authors during the ratification debates.

# VIII

## 1789–1794

# Power of the Purse

GEORGE WASHINGTON CAME INTO OFFICE ALMOST PREAPPROVED, A vast majority anticipating that this known and proven leader would be their president. When selecting his chief executive officers, Washington in turn sought out proven men. After serving as minister to France for four years, Thomas Jefferson was to be secretary of state, while Henry Knox would stay on as secretary of war, the position he held under the Articles of Confederation. Edmund Randolph, Virginia's attorney general for a decade, served the entire country in an identical posting.

## WASHINGTON CHOOSES HIS MAN

The secretary of the treasury would need to shore up the nation's faltering finances, taking on a task that dwarfed all others. Eight years earlier,

OPPOSITE: Engraving of Alonzo Chappel's portrait of Hamilton

with the nation flat broke, Robert Morris, then the superintendent of finance, had offered his own personal credit as collateral for the nation's, a stratagem that worked. Washington would be negligent if he did not ask "The Financier" to serve again. But Morris was more of a businessman than a statesman, and his true joy, one might even say his art, was making money. He declined.

Washington turned next to Hamilton, never doubting his brilliance, dedication, and work ethic. During the war, his former aide had penned notes in his pay books on trade, banking, investment, geography, and exchange rates, and he had gone on to serve under Morris. Hamilton seemed a natural fit, but would he take the job? His friends counseled against it. Gouverneur Morris warned him off for a solid reason—he'd be personally responsible for levying new taxes, and what could make him less popular? Robert Troup, Hamilton's roommate at King's College and an ongoing confidante and business consultant, noted that a paltry governmental salary would not sustain a household that included his wife, Elizabeth, seven-year-old Philip, five-year old Angelica, three-year-old Alexander Jr., and one-year-old James Alexander.

Both advisers would prove correct but Hamilton ignored all counsel. Popularity meant nothing to him. His aim was to make the federal government as strong as possible, to give it the highest "tone" allowable under the new Constitution. His new role could allow him to realize that goal. And by taking the job he demonstrated, for better or worse, that he cared more about the nation's finances than his family's.

Although Hamilton technically did not outrank the rest of Washington's administrators, in practice he became the second most powerful official in America. John Adams, the vice president, had no mandated executive responsibilities. Washington expected Jefferson, Knox, and Randolph to implement designated strategies, much as his officers had done

This profile portrait of Hamilton is one of a number of replicas attributed to the artist William J. Weaver, after either a bust or print of Hamilton, as Weaver did not have a life sitting with the statesman

in wartime. On the other hand, Washington recognized that only a man with great financial proficiency could put the struggling nation on its feet, and he did not trust his own capacity in that field. He required Hamilton's expertise, and so would carefully attend to his advice. Subject only to the approval of Congress and his former commander's assent, Hamilton was to have free rein, as no other man did. Back in 1780, in his letter to James Duane, Hamilton had written: *"that power, which holds the purse strings absolutely, must rule."*[1] Those strings were now his. During the war, as the commander in chief's right-hand man, he had been *close* to power; as secretary of the treasury, he *held* power.

## WALL STREET VERSUS MAIN STREET: HAMILTON'S FINANCIAL PLAN

Without delay, on September 11, 1789, the Senate confirmed Hamilton's appointment. Immediately, the House of Representatives instructed him to devise a plan "for the support of the public credit, as a matter of high importance to the national honor and prosperity."[2] Days later Congress adjourned, not to meet again for more than three months. The treasury secretary could not adjourn—he alone had to calculate how much the nation owed and conjure up a repayment plan. Hamilton had been struggling with this very problem since 1781, when he outlined a financial plan to Robert Morris. Although he did not have to start from scratch, he did have to amass and assemble an astounding array of new data.

By the time Congress returned to work in the early days of 1790, Hamilton had it all worked out. The federal government owed $54 million while state governments owed another $25 million, huge debt totals for the time. The United States would assume the debts of individual states; whoever held a state note could trade it in for a new federal one. All debts would be honored, but they would not all be redeemed at once. The government would establish a special "sinking fund" dedicated to redeeming some notes on a regular basis while paying a set quarterly interest on those outstanding. The regularity of the system would guarantee to investors,

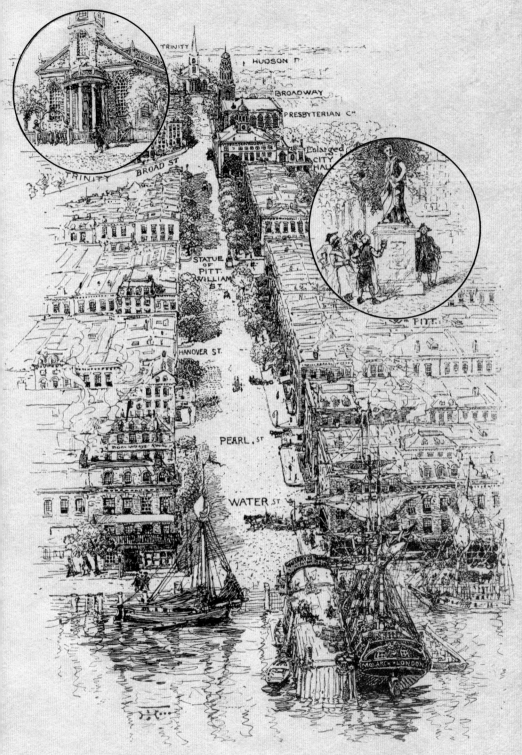

Bird's-eye view of Wall Street, about 1774

both at home and abroad, that the United States was good for its word and government notes would yield decent interest. "Public credit" would be restored.[3]

Naturally the scheme thrilled those who held notes, but others cried foul. During the Revolutionary War, Congress had paid many of its bills with notes instead of hard cash, which was in critically short supply. Soldiers who placed their lives on the line or farmers who supplied those soldiers wound up with mere certificates that could not be redeemed for years. Many of these recipients, needing real money for current expenses, had sold their notes to speculators for a small fraction of their face value. Now, if those notes were redeemed in full, those speculators, often wealthy to begin with, would reap windfall profits. A note yielding 6 percent interest on face value, but purchased for twenty cents on the dollar, would produce a 30 percent annual interest on the investment, and when the note was finally paid off, it would yield a 500 percent profit. James Madison, among many others, suggested that speculators get back only what they had shelled out.

A speculator's bonanza came at the taxpayers' expense, no less. To pay interest and redeem the notes in full, Hamilton proposed excise taxes "upon wines, distilled spirits, teas and coffees." He detailed thirty such taxes, including:

> Upon every gallon of Madeira Wine, of the quality of London particular, thirty-five cents. . .
> Upon every gallon of distilled Spirits, more than ten per cent. below proof, according to Dicas's hydrometer, twenty cents. . .
> Upon every pound of Souchong and other black Teas, except Bohea, twenty cents. . .
> Upon every pound of Coffee, five cents.[4]

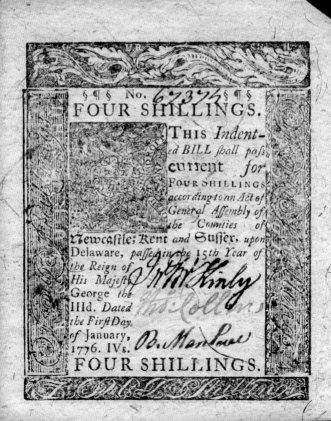

Early American currency

These were "pernicious luxuries," he pronounced, which were "consumed in so great abundance" that they produced "national extravagance and impoverishment." Liquor was worst of all. "The consumption of ardent spirits particularly, no doubt very much on account of their cheapness, is carried to an extreme, which is truly to be regretted, as well in regard to the health and the morals, as to the economy of the community." Taxing spirits would simultaneously fund the national debt and improve the nation's morals.

**ABOVE:** Originally designed as the Philadelphia County Courthouse, Congress Hall at the corner of Sixth and Chestnut served as the seat of the U.S. Congress from 1790 to 1800.

The tax on spirits proved wildly unpopular west of the Appalachian Mountains. Farmers who turned grain into liquor for a living closed roads to impede the travel of taxmen, threatened collectors with humiliation and bodily harm, organized committees of correspondence, and erected liberty poles, all reminiscent of revolutionary days, when protestors vented about Parliament and King George III. Now they turned on Congress and Alexander Hamilton.

Anti-Federalists joined the fracas, fulminating against the federal assumption of state debts. If the federal government held, as Hamilton put it, "the purse strings absolutely," it would become too powerful. Taxpayers in Virginia, Maryland, North Carolina, and Georgia, states that had already retired most of their debts, groused too. Why should they now pay off debts incurred by *other* states?

Caught in the grassroots crossfire, Hamilton resorted to political ploys and maneuvers, his area of expertise. "Mr. Hamilton is very uneasy, as far as I can learn, about his funding system," noted William Maclay, an opposition senator from Pennsylvania. Hamilton "spent most of his time in running from place to place among the members," and he even deployed a minister to preach the merits of the financial plan "as if he had been in the pulpit." Maclay concluded, "Hamilton, literally speaking, is moving heaven and earth in favor of his system."[5]

Horse trading, not divine intervention, steered Hamilton's plan through Congress. To broker a deal, Thomas Jefferson staged a famous dinner party. One invitee, Madison, agreed to back away from his fierce opposition to the assumption of state debts if the other, Hamilton, persuaded Northerners to relocate the nation's capital in the South. Two groups were bought off. Congressmen from Virginia and Maryland, who were opposed to the assumption of state debts, instantly consented to it if the capital would be on the Potomac River, which divides those states.

In return, proponents of debt assumption from Pennsylvania withdrew their opposition to relocating the capital. There was one caveat; for the first ten years Philadelphia was to be the nation's capital. Such was politics, same as it ever was.

# A NATIONAL BANK: DOWN TO THE WIRE

By 1790 Robert Morris's Bank of North America had essentially been privatized, its federal ties severed. But late that year, Hamilton proposed a successor. This "Bank of the United States" would operate under the government's aegis and issue notes that could circulate as currency. Private investors would purchase four-fifths of the stock, with the government holding the remainder. That start-up money, along with funds from depositors, could then be invested in roads, canals, and harbors—what we call infrastructure and people at the time called internal improvements. Hamilton viewed the bank as serving the national interest; others saw it as centralized control and a takeover by the moneyed class. Despite public outcry, Hamilton's bank bill breezed through the Federalist-controlled Congress. Nonetheless, its passage posed a new, critical question—did Congress have the authority to mandate a national bank? Could it exercise a power not specifically authorized by the Constitution?

The legislation required presidential approval, and three of Washington's closest advisors—Jefferson, Randolph, and Madison—advised a veto. They claimed that Congress had indeed exceeded its Constitutional mandate. Washington asked for Hamilton's input "as soon as is convenient."[6] *Soon* was the operative word; according to the Constitution, a president had only ten days to either sign or veto a bill. Since he had received the bank bill at noon on Monday, February 14, it would seem that Washington only had until noon on Thursday, February 24, to make up his mind.

Hamilton received Washington's request on February 16, which gave him eight days to argue the case for the bank he envisioned. A lot was at stake. Although never at a loss for words, he was challenged by the tight deadline. He worked at an impassioned pace, but on Monday, February 21 —day seven—he requested Washington's "indulgence for not having yet finished." He was "anxious to give the point a *thorough examination*" and could not conclude his assignment "before Tuesday or Wednesday *morning* early."[7] That would be day nine, which was cutting it very close. But might there be wiggle room?

Washington asked Hamilton for a "legal interpretation of the constitution"—what did that document mean by "ten days"?[8] In Hamilton's opinion Sundays did not count. That gave Washington until Friday, not Thursday, to decide. Hamilton also appended a few hours. So long as "Congress are sitting," Washington could ignore the noon deadline and hand in his decision later in the day.[9] Although Hamilton was his secretary of the treasury, not his attorney general, Washington accepted this answer as authoritative.

When submitting his lengthy argument on Wednesday, Hamilton admitted he had labored "the greatest part of last night" to finish it. Any student can identify with Hamilton here, but this was no ordinary term paper. The very scope of the government was at stake. Certain constitutional powers, although not stated, were *implied*, he maintained. Since the Constitution empowered Congress to manage finances, and since a national bank was a necessary means to that end, Congress had the authority, an *implied* authority, to establish one.

Hamilton's persuasive, legalistic justifications for the bill are part and parcel of the public record. There was also a pragmatic case to be made and chances are he made it—though no one was privy to the conversation— when he personally badgered Washington on Thursday from early

This 1923 illustration depicts Hamilton, at a cabinet meeting, urging Washington not to veto the bill establishing the Bank of the United States. Note redheaded Thomas Jefferson sulking as Hamilton holds forth. We do not know if such a meeting took place, but we do know that Hamilton visited Washington at the last minute to hammer home his points.

morning until two in the afternoon. For years he and Washington had pushed for a strong, efficient national government, he likely contended, and they and their fellow nationalists had gained ground by framing, ratifying, and implementing the Constitution. A narrow interpretation of congressional power would cede that ground. A veto was a retreat. On Friday, February 25—the eleventh day, not the tenth, but by Hamilton's calculation legally acceptable—Washington signed the bank bill.

## "An Embryo Caesar"

Late in January 1791, while Congress was considering the bank bill, Hamilton received shocking news from New York. Through backroom deals, Aaron Burr had unseated Hamilton's father-in-law, the incumbent Philip Schuyler, for a seat in the United States Senate.

The paths of Hamilton and Burr first diverged in 1787 during the fierce debates on the new Constitution. As Hamilton fought relentlessly for ratification, Burr sat on the sidelines, saying not a word. Hamilton judged him "equivocal" but suspected him of being a closet Anti-Federalist.[10] Burr's fence-straddling soon paid off. The man who had alienated no one while astride that fence was made New York's attorney general in 1789, appointed by Governor Clinton, a strident proponent of state's rights, especially New York's own. In less than two years, in 1791, Burr was selected as the challenger in a campaign for the federal Senate seat held by Philip Schuyler. In a close contest, Burr prevailed by a mere five votes in the New York Assembly, which chose the state's two senators. Schuyler took the result in stride: "As no good could possibly result from evincing any resentment to Mr. Burr for the part he took last winter," he wrote to Hamilton, "I have on every Occasion behaved towards him as If he had never been the principal in the business."[11] Hamilton was not so resigned. He suspected, correctly, that an alliance of factions, unhappy with his audacious financial program, had unseated Schuyler to strike back. Aaron Burr was rising at a meteoric clip.

Less than two years later his name was again put forward when political insiders determined to challenge another incumbent, John Adams, the vice president. Burr and Governor Clinton became the principal contenders. Even though Clinton was an Anti-Federalist, Hamilton thought him a man "of probity" in his private life. By contrast, he judged

Burr "unprincipled both as a public and private man. . . . He is for or against nothing, but as it suits his interest or ambition." Burr aimed to put himself, Hamilton said, "at the head of what he calls the 'popular party.'" But if he was flying under the banner of "Liberty," it was only because "he knows as well as most men how to make use of the name." This was the sport of tyrants. Hamilton concluded, "If we have an embryo Caesar in the United States, 'tis Burr." The upstart had to be stopped, and Hamilton was the one to do it: "I feel it a religious duty to oppose his career."[12]

## WASHINGTON'S CABINET: AN INTRAMURAL DIVIDE

If Hamilton faced one adversary in New York, he faced a far more consequential one in Philadelphia, Thomas Jefferson. Jefferson had hazel eyes and reddish hair and stood tall but without the commanding presence of a George Washington—"[H]is whole figure has a loose, shackling air," said one observer.[13] He was unassuming in his affect but had amassed an impressive résumé. He was lead author of the Declaration of Independence; former governor of the nation's largest state, Virginia; minister to the young nation's principal ally, France; and now Washington's secretary of state.

Hamilton and Jefferson had never met before they cohabited in Washington's "cabinet," a term just coming into use that designated the president's chief advisors. There was as yet no bad blood between them. That soon changed. First, the secretary of state opposed a measure the secretary of the treasury introduced during debate on the national bank. Next, Hamilton returned the favor two years later by intervening in Jefferson's realm when Britain and France were at war.

Some Americans, like Hamilton, favored Britain, looking to a shared language and culture and to close commercial ties. Others, such as Jefferson,

Washington delivering his inaugural address April 1789, in New York's old City Hall

favored France, a country that had come to the aid of Americans during the Revolutionary War. Following suit in a revolution of its own, France now struggled for "Liberté, égalité, fraternité." Even after Jefferson learned of the September Massacre of 1792—when Parisian Jacobins guillotined one thousand prisoners—he sprang to the defense of the executioners. In a revolution, as in war, some innocents must fall because "it was necessary to use the arm of the people." That arm was "a machine not quite so blind as balls and bombs, but blind to a certain degree." The ends justified the means: "The liberty of the whole earth was depending on the issue of the contest, and was ever such a prize won with so little innocent blood?"[14]

Hamilton had always preferred strong rules to mob rule. Just as he opposed mobs in revolutionary America, he opposed the French ones

now. To Hamilton's way of thinking, even in something as intrinsically violent as war, honorable men subscribed to rules of engagement. A good commander did not allow his men to jeer the defeated or desecrate bodies, for example. Following this law-abiding spirit, Hamilton elaborated rules for revolution as well. It had to be "a *free*, *regular*, and *deliberate* act of the nation, and with such a spirit of justice and humanity, as ought to silence all scruples about the validity of what has been done."[15] America's revolution, having met the standard, deserved to be celebrated. The standard didn't seem to be holding in France, however, as revolutionaries purged and slaughtered their opponents, even guillotining King Louis XVI and stuffing his head between his legs.

Washington tried to keep America out of the war fought between European nations. On April 22, 1793, he issued an executive proclamation pledging the United States to "pursue a conduct friendly and impartial toward the belligerent powers" and forbidding American citizens from aiding or abetting the hostile actions of either power.[16] Using the pen name "Pacificus," Hamilton supported the president in a series of letters to the press. In one, he claimed that the executive, not the legislature, was the sole *"organ of intercourse between the nation and foreign nations."*[17]

Secretary of State Jefferson fumed. The "hotheaded" and "disrespectful" secretary of the treasury favored dangerously "dictatorial" executive authority. Since it was bad form for one of Washington's secretaries to attack another, Jefferson leaned on James Madison: "For god's sake, my dear Sir, take up your pen, select the most striking heresies, and cut him to pieces in the face of the public." Madison complied. Writing as "Helvidius," a Roman statesman allied with Brutus and Cassius, he countered each of Pacificus's letters.[18]

OPPOSITE: Rembrandt Peale's official presidential portrait of Thomas Jefferson (1800)

Washington arriving at Congress Hall in Philadelphia for his second presidential inauguration on March 4, 1793

Only five years earlier, when these two opponents had collaborated as "Publius," Hamilton had said that foreign affairs were "more of the legislative than of the executive character," and that it was "*utterly unsafe and improper . . . to commit interests of so delicate and momentous a kind, as those which concern its intercourse with the rest of the world, to the . . . President of the United States.*"[19] Back then, he wanted to convince a wary public that presidential power was limited, but now he was the president's right-hand man. Just as he had done at the Constitutional Convention, he exalted executive authority.

Hamilton's arguments prevailed and Washington's proclamation of neutrality stood. But with each defeat, Jefferson's animosity intensified. When Hamilton contracted yellow fever in the 1793 epidemic that killed some five thousand Philadelphians, Jefferson wrote to Madison, accusing

Hamilton of being as "timid in sickness" as he was "on horseback" or "on the water" and saying that "his friends, who have not seen him, suspect it is only an autumnal fever he has."[20] Jefferson made the most of any opportunity to cast aspersions on the man he openly despised.

Late in 1793, Jefferson resigned from his position as secretary of state. "I am then to be liberated from the hated occupations of politics, and to sink into the bosom of my family, my farm and my books," he wrote to Angelica Schuyler Church, whom he had met, and flirted with, in Paris.[21] But Jefferson told Edmund Randolph he intended to make one exception after retreating to private life: "I indulge myself on one political topic only, that is, in [dis]closing to my countrymen the shameless corruption" of certain members of Congress who display an "implicit devotion to the treasury."[22] For his part, Hamilton questioned Jefferson's alleged retirement altogether. "'Tis evident beyond a question, from every movement, that Mr. Jefferson aims with ardent desire at the Presidential Chair," he prophesized.[23]

Two parties were forming, one with Hamilton at the head, the other led by Jefferson. One favored commercial development. The other suspected commercial interests of corruption and favored rural interests and hardworking "yeomen" or farmers. The "spirit of party," which the framers of the Constitution had decried, was consuming the nation's civic life.

## "WHISKEY REBELS"

By the summer of 1794, protests against Hamilton's tax on liquor reached a fever pitch in Kentucky and in the western regions of Maryland, Virginia, and the Carolinas. Pennsylvania faced a full-scale rebellion from protesters who called themselves "Regulators"—they wanted to regulate alleged abuses, like Hamilton's tax on spirits. Jefferson dubbed

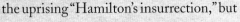

the uprising "Hamilton's insurrection," but
Hamilton won the spin game with
"Whiskey Rebellion," a derogatory
label that has stuck to this day.

Insurgents initiated plans
to secede from the Union and
marched under a flag of their own.
It bore six stripes, one for each of four
rebellious counties in Pennsylvania and
two for those in northwestern Virginia.

On August 1, 1794, an estimated 6,000 to 9,000 of these rebels
made a show of force at Braddock's Field, site of a famous battle in the
French and Indian War. Hamilton urged Washington to quash
the rebellion with military force. Washington did not relish the idea
of an American army advancing on its citizens, certainly not until
all legal avenues were exhausted. He asked a Supreme Court justice,
Pennsylvania's James Wilson, if there were any further legal actions
he could take, short of military suppression. Wilson said there were not.

The rebellion continued for two months until finally, on September 30, the president, with Hamilton by his side, headed westward with
12,950 militiamen from four states. At first sight of this massive force,
larger than the Continental Army during much of the Revolutionary War,
the insurgents backed down. The message delivered to all Americans was
simple and clear—the American Revolution was over. There would be no

ABOVE: Supreme Court justice James Wilson, whose 1794 opinion supported Hamilton's
aggressive military response to the Whiskey Rebellion. OPPOSITE: An orderly book from
the Whiskey Rebellion. FOLLOWING: Donna Neary's painting shows Washington, with
Hamilton (far right), inspecting the troops before marching into western Pennsylvania.

7

General departments, who are requested that all regimental returns conform thereto. The Articles of War must be read by the Captains to their respective companies, and fully explained to the men,

In future the Issuing of Provisions and Forage will commence at four o'Clock in the afternoon, Close at five; one hour is fully sufficient for this business, if the expected punctuality of the several officers takes place. On reference to the Commissions of the officers of the Cavalry and to the Principles established by the Government of Virginia for the settlement of Rank; it appears the Captain Lewis is the Senior officer of the Virginia Corps of horse he will of course take upon himself the duties heretofore assigned to the Senior officer of each corps of Dragoons.

The Quarter Master General will be pleased to provide proper houses, for the reception of the sick, together with all stores necessary for their accommodation and comfort

The President has been pleased to appoint Col.o Presley Nevill Paymaster General, he is to be respected accordingly

By the Commander in Chief

Thomas Nelson Adj.t Gen.l pro tem

Head Quarters fort Cumberland October 14th 1794.

General Orders

As soon as the Maryland line under Brigadier Gen.l Smith join, which will take Place this Evening or Tomorrow Morning the Adjutant General will be pleased to commence the System to be permanently observed with respect to Camp duties of every Sort; the particular rules & forms will be found in the treatise entitled Regulations for the Order and Discipline of the troops of the United States. A picquet consisting of the Same number as composed the one in front, will be established in the rear one Quarter of a mile below the Cavalry incampment

repeat performances. This new government, embodied under the authority of the people themselves, would enforce its laws.

Many Americans derided a military action directed at fellow citizens, and as Hamilton returned to Philadelphia from Pittsburgh, an escort of six soldiers protected him from possible assailants. "It is long since I have learnt to hold popular opinion of no value," he told Washington.[24] The president too was the subject of criticism. Edmund Randolph told him "how much Colonel Hamilton's accompanying him was talked of out of doors, and how much stress was laid upon the seeming necessity of the Commander-in-Chief having him always at his elbow."[25]

## STEPPING DOWN

Popular or not, Hamilton, with Washington's backing, had prevailed on nearly every contested issue. In June 1793, he had told the president he planned to resign, but he then put off his departure "until the clouds over our affairs, which have come on so fast of late, shall be dispersed"—an allusion to the Whiskey Rebellion.[26] On December 1, 1794, after it was suppressed, he informed Washington that he would leave office two months hence. This time he kept his word.

Shortly after retiring, Hamilton received a letter from his long-lost paternal uncle William Hamilton, living in Scotland. In reply, Alexander rendered a fair summary of his achievements:

> After the peace, I settled in the City of New York in the practice of the law; and was in a very lucrative course of practice, when the derangement of our public affairs, by the feebleness of the general confederation, drew me again reluctantly into public life. I became a member of the Convention which framed the present Constitution of

the U States; and having taken part in this measure, I conceived myself to be under an obligation to lend my aid towards putting the machine in some regular motion. Hence I did not hesitate to accept the offer of President Washington to undertake the office of Secretary of the Treasury.

In that office, I met with many intrinsic difficulties, and many artificial ones proceeding from passions, not very worthy, common to human nature, and which act with peculiar force in republics. The object, however, was effected, of establishing public credit and introducing order into the finances.[27]

In his autobiographical summary, he spoke of the "reflections of prudence in relation to a growing family." It was time to care for that family. Politics had lost its appeal, or so he told himself, but try as he might, he wasn't one to hover on the sidelines and watch others play the game.

# IX

## 1795–1799

# Politics and Scandal

On July 18, 1795, the former secretary of the treasury, now a private citizen, mounted a stoop near Federal Hall to join in a debate being held, as was said in the day, "out-of-doors," a venue that was also out of Alexander Hamilton's comfort zone. Accustomed to speaking "within chambers" before gentlemen like himself, he now faced a raucous crowd of New Yorkers from all different classes. He urged "the necessity of a full discussion before the citizens could form their opinions," but opinions already seemed formed. Their "hissings, coughings, and hootings" stopped him cold.[1] Next, "stones were thrown at Mr. Hamilton one of which grazed his head."[2] A disgruntled Federalist, taking Hamilton's side, noted that the protestors "were prudent to endeavor to knock out Hamilton's brains, to reduce him to an equality with themselves," brainless in other words.[3] Both sides, in their own way, expressed impassioned sentiments.

Why such fury?

**OPPOSITE:** John Trumbull's portrait of Hamilton (1832)

# OUT-OF-DOORS

Late in 1793 and early in 1794, British ships seized almost 250 American vessels and reportedly mistreated many of the captured seamen. Britain justified the practice by claiming that the United States was trading with France, an enemy nation, but that did not quell the popular outrage. In retaliation the House of Representatives overwhelmingly passed a nonimportation bill that punished Britain by inhibiting her commerce with America. As an admirer of Britain who vigorously promoted trade with her, Hamilton was horrified by the legislation. Just before the House bill arrived at the Senate, Hamilton convinced Washington to address American grievances by dispatching a rescue mission to London. The president agreed and tapped John Jay, chief justice of the Supreme Court and Hamilton's former collaborator on *The Federalist* project, to lead it.

The treaty that Jay negotiated normalized trade with Britain while prohibiting trade with France. Britain agreed to repay American merchants for the recently seized ships and merchandise but would not free the seamen, who potentially could be impressed into British service. Prosperous merchants and Hamilton were pleased. Great numbers of other Americans were not. So it was that Hamilton faced "a numerous body of citizens collected at 12 o'clock on Saturday, at the Federal Hall." They were protesting the Jay Treaty, which had yet to be ratified by the United States Senate.[4]

Rebuffed by the crowd, Hamilton stormed off. He soon encountered two men of his class, but of differing political persuasions, and they engaged in an "altercation." When Hamilton interjected, one, James Nicholson, called him "an Abettor of Tories." Far worse, he stated that Hamilton had once "declined an interview"—code at the time for shunning a duel. A man who did that was forever after known as a coward. Hamilton, who was always very mindful of his reputation,

This illustration of a protest against the "Jay Treaty" shows John Jay being burned in effigy.

defended himself from the accusation, declaring, "No man could affirm that with truth." Then, as any gentleman must do on such an occasion, he pledged "to convince Mr. Nicholson of his mistake"—in other words, settle the matter with their own duel. Nicholson accepted the challenge.[5] The day was not done. For some unknown reason, Hamilton joined in a social function at the house of Edward Livingston, where gentlemen on both sides were contesting the treaty issue. In the heat of the moment, Hamilton declared that "if the parties were to contend in a Personal way"—yet another code for dueling—he was "ready to fight the Whole *'Detestable faction'* one by one." Stepping forward, Edward's law partner Maturin Livingston said "that he accepted the challenge & would meet him in half an hour where he pleased." Hamilton replied, saying "he had one on his Hands already & when that was settled he would call on him." Edward, who reported the happenings at his house to his mother, concluded: "I mention this Circumstance particularly that you may Judge how much he [Hamilton] must be Mortified at his loss of Influence before he would descend to language that would become a Street Bully."[6]

In the end, Hamilton dueled with neither James Nicholson nor Maturin Livingston. Tempers calmed, as was common. For every duel fought at that time perhaps a dozen or a score or several score of challenges were offered and accepted. The *language* of dueling, more than duels themselves, afforded a man the honor he sought. Hamilton understood that language far better than the crowd of commoners' hissing and hooting and rock hurling—for him a foreign tongue—and reverted to it twice on the same day, perhaps with some sense of relief at being fully comprehended.

## INFLUENCE AND INTRIGUE

Washington never broke with his habit of consulting with Hamilton. A request made seven months after Hamilton's departure, which had nothing to do with finance, is typical:

> "Altho' you are not in the Administration—a thing I sincerely regret—I must, nevertheless, (knowing how intimately acquainted you are with all the concerns of this country) request the favor of you to note down such occurrences as, in your opinion are proper subjects for communication to Congress at their next Session."[7]

Washington continued to ask for Hamilton's advice on foreign policy, the purview of the secretary of state, or on interpretations of the Constitution, rightly the attorney general's province. When Hamilton said one thing but cabinet members advised otherwise, the president sided with Hamilton. It isn't surprising that Hamilton drafted Washington's Farewell Address, which the president delivered with only slight modifications.

In his final message to the nation, Washington championed the "unity of government" and urged "respect for its authority, compliance with its laws, [and] acquiescence in its measures." He warned that unity was threatened by "obstructions to the execution of the laws," an obvious reference to the recent insurgency in western Pennsylvania, and by "combinations and associations" that acted "covertly and insidiously" to "counteract" the existing government—an allusion to Democratic-Republican societies that had sprung up to oppose policies of the current administration.[8]

The Farewell Address seems today no more than a reasonable plea to avoid political quarrels. But at the time, adversaries read it as a Hamiltonian justification of Federalist policies and tantamount to a battle cry. Fisher Ames, a diehard Massachusetts Federalist, enunciated a common contemporaneous assessment. "It will serve as a signal, like dropping a hat, for the party racers to start, and I expect a great deal of noise, whipping, and spurring."[9]

The race was on to determine President Washington's successor, but who would be the "party racers"?

Republicans selected an eminent, high-ranking figure and former secretary of state who derided the Federalist administration: Thomas Jefferson. John Adams was Washington's heir-apparent but, lacking charisma, he had few die-hard fans. Southerners looked at Adams and saw a stalwart New Englander; there was little in the way of spontaneous attraction. Others saw a temperamental, crabby man who liked British-style monarchy a little too well.

Hamilton and Adams were not collegial, nor were they yet sworn enemies. But Hamilton recognized a dire truth. During Washington's administration, he had been close to the epicenter of power and influence. Under Adams he would have no place at all, and he wasn't one to quietly cede his place. Abetted by a cohort of insiders, he hatched a scheme. Nominally, they would enlist support for an Adams presidency but would then back Thomas Pinckney as vice-president. Pinckney, who hailed from South Carolina, could draw Southern votes and he was currently in the public eye. He had also just negotiated a widely popular treaty with Spain, securing rights to the Mississippi River.

By the rules set down in the Constitution, electors from each state would choose two candidates without distinguishing between them. The winner became the president, the runner-up, vice president. It was possible to game this system. If a party put forth two candidates, but one or two electors chose *not* to vote for the top pick, the vice-presidential candidate would emerge victorious. Hamilton had noted this in the very first election, back in 1789: "Every body is aware of that defect in the constitution which renders it possible that the man intended for Vice President may in fact turn up President."[10] During that election, he encouraged electors to leave Adams off their ballots so he could not "overtake" Washington. Now, he gamed the election again. He urged all Northern electors to include Pinckney on their tickets, while expecting that a few Southern electors would leave off Adams. This was self-serving. If Pinckney became president, he would owe his office to Hamilton and his friends, but if

OPPOSITE: Portrait of Major General Thomas Pinckney, by John Trumbull

Adams prevailed, he would have earned it in his own right. In the words of Hamilton confidant Robert Troup, "we [will] have Mr. Pinckney completely in our power."[11]

The scheme backfired. No Federalists in the South "threw away" votes for Adams, but several Northern Federalists left off Pinckney so he would not beat out Adams. This produced a very strange result: Adams, with seventy-one electoral votes, became president, while Jefferson beat out Pinckney for second place, sixty-eight to fifty-nine. For the only time in our nation's history, the president and vice president were from competing political parties. A Federalist was at the helm, a Republican his supposed helpmate. The relationship could be nothing but fractious and taxing.

When Abigail Adams realized what Hamilton had done and what was coming, she wrote to her husband, the president-elect: "I have often said to you, H——n is a Man ambitious as Julius Ceasar, a subtle intriguer. . . . I have ever kept My Eye upon him. He has obtain'd a great influence over some of the most worthy and amiable of our acquaintance."[12]

John wrote back to Abigail: "Hamilton I know to be . . . as great an Hypocrite as any in the U.S. His Intrigues in the Election I despise. That he has Talents I admit but I dread none of them. I shall take no notice of his Puppy head but retain the same Opinion of him I always had and maintain the same Conduct towards him I always did, that is keep him at a distance."[13] Countless others in political echelons now considered

Abigail Adams

Hamilton a "subtle intriguer" and thought it best to "keep him at a distance." Because of his personal miscalculations, he now had less leverage, not more. In the following year that debit would mount exponentially, once again through his own hand.

## Dishonor

In the prior decade, rebuffing his political enemies, Hamilton launched a third-person defense: "Mr. Hamilton can however defy all their malevolent ingenuity to produce a single instance of his conduct public, or private, inconsistent with the strictest rules of integrity and honor."[14] In this decade, he sacrificed integrity and honor and laid the sacrifice at the public's feet.

In 1797 he released a pamphlet, and a confession. "Sometime in the summer of the year 1791, a woman called at my house in the city of Philadelphia." According to Hamilton, the woman, Maria Reynolds, claimed that her husband James Reynolds had treated her cruelly and left her for another woman. Maria, now supposedly alone and without means to support herself, needed money to return to New York City where she could live with friends. She wept. She implored:

> In the evening I put a bank-bill in my pocket and went to the house. I enquired for Mrs. Reynolds and was shown up stairs, at the head of which she met me and conducted me into a bedroom. I took the bill out of my pocket and gave it to her. Some conversation ensued, from which it was quickly apparent that other than pecuniary consolation would be acceptable. After this I had frequent meetings with her, most of them at my own house; Mrs. Hamilton with her children being absent on a visit to her father.[15]

When Eliza told Hamilton she would soon return from Albany, he advised her not to "hurry so as to injure either yourself or the children."[16] When she did return, he continued to look in on Maria at her lodgings, even as his wife was pregnant with their fifth child.

The entanglement lasted over a year. At its inception Maria was twenty-three and Hamilton thirty-four. On the political front, the usual worries and encumbrances hemmed him in. At home there was love and felicity but also all the common, diminutive day-to-day marital transactions. Four children ran about, their prattle and demands more diminutive still. Hamilton had fought against the restraints of ordinary life before by courting danger in warfare, impulse overtaking reason.

When, unexpectedly, Maria made her appearance, the histrionics of her appeal must have seemed like a possible release from habit and routine—if he dared charge forward. He did. Whenever he tried to escape, Maria reeled him back in with letters like this one: "Sir Rest assuirred I will never ask you to Call on me again I have kept my Bed those tow dayes and now rise from My pillow wich your Neglect has filled with the sharpest thorns."[17] In one fell swoop, and in barely more than thirty words, Maria Reynolds supposedly released Hamilton, her lover, saying she would ask no more of him. She next tempted him back with "bed" and "pillow," blamed him for neglecting her, and suffered before his eyes from love and desperate need of him. Full to the brim with pathos and high romance, the note appealed to the male ego, the male organ, and misplaced gallantry. Hamilton was susceptible.

Despite Maria's claims of abandonment, James Reynolds apparently operated behind the scenes from start to finish. In due course there were threats and requests for sums. Hamilton's $1,000 offering was followed by smaller ones. He was not only an easy mark for a man prostituting a wife, but politically vulnerable. Politics reared its head when Jacob Clingman, a friend of Reynolds, observed Hamilton departing the Reynolds household on one occasion and entering it on another. Clingman heard both Maria and James say that they had had financial transactions with Hamilton. It might have ended there except Clingman and Reynolds were caught in an underhanded swindling scheme, charged, and jailed.

Clingman had once clerked for the speaker of the house, Frederick Muhlenberg, who helped negotiate his release on a promise to make reparations. Now he hinted to Muhlenberg of Hamilton's dark doings, and

Pennsylvania Congressman Frederick Muhlenberg, who played an important early role in the Reynolds scandal

# OBSERVATIONS

ON

## CERTAIN DOCUMENTS

CONTAINED IN NO. V & VI OF

## " THE HISTORY OF THE UNITED STATES
### FOR THE YEAR 1796,"

IN WHICH THE

### *CHARGE OF SPECULATION*

AGAINST

# ALEXANDER HAMILTON,

LATE SECRETARY OF THE TREASURY,

## IS FULLY REFUTED.

WRITTEN BY HIMSELF.

PHILADELPHIA:
PRINTED FOR JOHN FENNO, BY JOHN BIOREN.
1797.

Muhlenberg pursued the matter. He and Virginia senator James Monroe visited James Reynolds, still in jail, and then Maria. On December 12, 1792, armed with stories, insinuations, unsigned scraps of paper, and a few letters, these two men, along with Representative Abraham B. Venable, called on Hamilton. He must have blanched at the sight of them, and especially at the sight of Monroe. If the thought was to bring him down, this confederate of Jefferson and Madison, his political adversaries, might do just that.

Hamilton did not deny the allegations but instead implored the men to return that night. When they did, incredibly, he placed evidence before them—letters from James and Maria Reynolds. These cleared him of accusations of duplicitous financial dealing, he asserted. He was but an adulterer. Unsuccessful and embarrassed, they tried to halt Hamilton's angry, rambling admissions. Alleging they would take it no further and promising to maintain silence forever, they left his house, the incriminating letters in hand. At Hamilton's request copies were made and delivered back to him.

Soon after, Maria Reynolds accused her husband of adultery and filed for divorce. Aaron Burr was her lawyer. Yet again, Burr's life and Hamilton's crisscrossed.

The matter seemed to be over and done with, but in 1797, when Hamilton's political stock was plummeting, a scurrilous pamphleteer and muckraker jumped in. The Scotsman James Thomas Callender, who specialized in character assassination, had obtained the letters entrusted to Monroe and company, possibly through the clerk who had copied them. He revealed all in a pamphlet that embraced speculations on financial corruption. The nightmare resurfaced for all to see.

OPPOSITE: Title page of the "Reynolds Pamphlet," in which Hamilton admits to his affair but counters charges of corruption

Friends at this point advised silence. Hamilton could say simply that congressmen had found him innocent of corruption charges six years before and end it there. But instead, frantic, he took himself off to a Philadelphia boardinghouse, far from Eliza. Between mad bouts of writing, he must have paced back and forth, floorboards creaking under his feet. In bed he woke often to stare at the dark. Come daylight, he scratched again at the papers on the table in front of him, describing the tawdry affair and blackmail. What emerged from all this was a ninety-eight-page pamphlet that Hamilton entitled *Observations on Certain Documents . . . In Which the Charge of Speculation Against Alexander Hamilton, Late Secretary of the Treasury, is Fully Refuted*—usually called, for obvious reasons, the Reynolds pamphlet.[18]

Often enough, and since his days on Nevis and St. Croix, Hamilton had reinvented himself. There was a Frankenstein-like element in the new self-fabrication; he was the man duped, the philanderer. But in creating that entity, he avoided the charge of political malfeasance. "The charge against me is a connection with one James Reynolds for purposes of improper monetary speculation," he wrote. "My real crime is an amorous connection with his wife. This confession is not made without a blush." He set out proof, which included twenty-two letters he had received from Maria Reynolds and James Reynolds and his complete correspondence with Monroe, Muhlenberg, and Venable. He insisted, however, that his public conduct remained consistent "with the strictest rules of integrity and honor," as he had proclaimed ten years earlier.

Gloating at what he had wrought, Callender wrote to Thomas Jefferson, saying "no anticipation can equal the infamy of this piece. It is worth all that fifty of the best pens in America could have said against him."[19] What Callender claimed was accurate, and the loss to Hamilton great. But though he seemed to self-immolate, his story was not done.

His tenacity, a signature trademark, yielded other chapters in his saga. Eliza was as tenacious, and the marriage was spared. The affair says much about Alexander's frailty. The durability of the marriage speaks to Eliza's strength.

After the pamphlet's publication in August, Washington sent a gift, a wine cooler. It was, he said, "a token of my sincere regard and friendship for you and a remembrance of me," and he signed, saying "and that you would be persuaded that with every sentiment of the highest regard, I remain your sincere friend and affectionate, honorable servant."[20] Not all reproached him, and not all was lost.

# A PHANTOM WAR

The following year America was roiled by a wave of anti-French sentiment, and Hamilton rode the wave, staging something of a comeback. Following the Jay Treaty, which reinvigorated Anglo-American commerce, France took a turn at raiding American ships, which were now trading with her enemy, Great Britain. This of course raised a popular clamor in the United States, which Hamilton fueled with a series of war-mongering diatribes he called "The Stand." In his view, the French Revolution, under the guise of "independence and liberty," had devolved into "the most flagitious, despotic and vindictive government that ever disgraced the annals of mankind." Comparing the "moderation" of Britain with the "inexorable arrogance" of France, he wrote:

> "My countrymen! can ye hesitate which to prefer? can ye consent to taste the brutalizing cup of disgrace, to wear the livery of foreign masters, to put on the hateful fetters of foreign bondage? . . . What is there to deter from the manful vindication of your rights and your honor?"[21]

Always fearful of mob rule, Hamilton had opposed the French Revolution at its outset in 1789. At that pivotal moment he shared his "foreboding of ill" with Lafayette, who had returned to France: "I dread the vehement character of your people, whom I fear you may find it more easy to bring on, than to keep within Proper bounds, after you have put them in motion."[22] But Lafayette embraced that revolution, much as he had the American Revolution, and with Jefferson's assistance drafted its central document, the *Déclaration des droits de l'homme et du citoyen* (*Declaration of the Rights of Man and of the Citizen*). Three years later, however, Lafayette soured on the wanton violence and tried to bolt to America. En route he was captured in Austria and locked up in one prison after another in perilous conditions. Angelica Church and her husband, John, hired an agent to help him escape, but he was recaptured.

Late in 1797, sickly and emaciated, Lafayette was finally released into the custody of an American consul in Hamburg. Normally, Hamilton would have ardently welcomed the return of his comrade to the United States, but not with anti-French rancor at a fever pitch. "'Tis most adviseable for you to remain in Europe 'till the difference is adjusted," he cautioned.[23]

For all the tough talk about war, the United States's army at that time could field only 4,000 soldiers, virtually all stationed along the nation's western borders. To prepare for a confrontation with France that many thought was imminent, Congress

Angelica Schuyler Church. Sister-in-law of Hamilton and wife of John Barker Church

Hamilton had always craved military honors, and in 1798, with the support of his mentor Washington, he finally became a general.

authorized an "Additional Army" of 10,000 men. Hamilton convinced George Washington to come out of retirement to head this force.[24]

Aging and increasingly infirm, Washington agreed to take charge only if he could approve the "principle Officers" and if he would not be "called into the field" until "it becomes indispensible by the urgency of circumstances."[25] Unwilling to trouble himself with the minutia of detail in recruiting, organizing, disciplining, and equipping an army, Washington wanted his former aide-de-camp to tend to all that. As acting commander, Hamilton would be second only to him. Writing to President John Adams, who alone had the constitutional authority to grant such appointments, he made his case:

> Although Colo. Hamilton has never acted in the character of a General Officer, yet his opportunities, as the principal & most confidential aid of the Commander in chief, afforded him the means of viewing every thing on a larger scale than those whose attentions were confined to Divisions or Brigades.[26]

Adams resented Washington's interference but, seeing no other choice, conceded. With a stroke of his pen he promoted "Colo. Hamilton," a man he intensely disliked, to major general, in command of all forces north of Virginia and west to the Mississippi River.

Initially, the work was mundane. From a small office on Greenwich Street in New York, aided only by twenty-year-old Philip Church, Angelica's son, he performed the necessary busywork, as Washington trusted him to do. His family told him that he suffered "from want of exercise" and warned "that this and unremitted Attention to business injures your health."[27]

But the mission was compelling and the rewards potentially vast. Hamilton envisioned an army not of 14,000 regular soldiers but 50,000, plus an additional 80,000 militiamen—and he lobbied for that increase.[28] The immediate purpose of this army-in-the-making was to prepare for war with France, but Hamilton, in his mind, escalated the war before it even began. Once the United States had beefed up its military forces, it might be able to wrest Florida and Louisiana from Spain, he suggested to political operatives in Congress.[29]

And why stop there? An international adventurer, Francisco de Miranda from Venezuela, tried to interest Hamilton in liberating Latin America. Hamilton took the bait, but in his reply to Miranda he enlisted his six-year-old son, John Church Hamilton, as penman to obfuscate his role if the letter fell into the wrong hands. He imagined a joint American-British force with the "principle agency" assigned to the United States—and "the command in this case would naturally fall upon me," he told Rufus King, his close political ally who was currently the nation's minister to Great Britain.[30]

Hamilton also asked Secretary of State Timothy Pickering to grant the country's verbal support to Toussaint Louverture, who had led a successful slave revolt in Haiti and hoped to liberate the slaves in neighboring Santo Domingo, still under French rule. Having grown up in the West Indies, however, Hamilton doubted whether a Caribbean society could sustain the republican principles that guided the United States. "No regular system of Liberty will at present suit St. Domingo," he explained. Getting far ahead of himself, he drafted a constitution for the yet-to-be nation that specified the "regular system" it should adopt—a "feudal system" in which a hereditary monarch enjoyed dictatorial powers over everything except the judicial system.[31]

Decades past, in those same feudal West Indies, Hamilton had dreamed of a war that would permit him to advance. He dreamed still and dreamed large. But his phantom army disappeared before it had fully formed when President John Adams dispatched a successful peace mission to France. War was not to be. After all was said and done, there was only a "Quasi-War," as textbooks call it, and a major general who never led more than a paper army.

# GEORGE WASHINGTON: IN MEMORIAM

As Hamilton prepared for war, Washington lived in peace at Mount Vernon. Almost daily he rode out on horseback to monitor work on his farms, ordinarily canvassing some twenty miles of land. On Thursday, December 12, 1799, he was caught in an afternoon storm, a mix of snow and hail and rain. He arrived back chilled, his clothes drenched. The next day he felt unwell yet paid no mind. But by Saturday morning there was no ignoring his unsettled breathing and painful throat. He had a blood letting at the hand of a trusted plantation overseer. Later, the family doctor, James Craik, bled him again. Before long, another doctor was sent for, and soon a third. The call-out signaled that Washington's state was dire. Early on Sunday afternoon he was bled for a last time, of a quart of blood.

Washington's secretary, Tobias Lear, chronicled his final hours. "About half past 4 o'clock" Washington asked Martha to bring him two wills; examining both, he chose the current one and asked that the other be burned. Around 5:00 pm he told Craik, "Doctor, I die hard; but I am not afraid to go." Minutes later, with all three doctors present, he thanked them for their "attentions" and asked that they "take no more trouble about me, let me go off quietly, I can not last long." Around 10:00 pm, as he faded, Washington made one last request. Aware of stories of premature

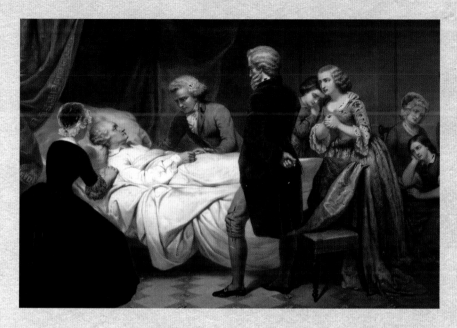

George Washington on his death bed attended by family and friends

burial, he called for Lear and told him, "Have me decently buried; and do not let my body be put into the Vault in less than three days after I am dead." Martha sat at the foot of the bed and servants surrounded it when he passed away. In the whole affair there was dignity, strength, attention to duty, and decorum. He died much as he lived.[32]

The last letter Washington wrote, two days before he died, was to Hamilton. Washington thanked him for his usual, exorbitantly detailed work on an enterprise prized by both men: a permanent military academy at West Point. It was the last of many dreams that the two had shared, with Hamilton working long into the night to make it a reality.

# X

# 1800–1804

# *Honor*

THE PRESIDENTIAL ELECTION OF 1800, LIKE THAT OF 1796, PITTED Federalist John Adams against Republican Thomas Jefferson. Once again, Jefferson was expected to carry the South and Adams most of the North, the electoral vote split evenly between them. New York was an anomaly, a "swing state" in today's parlance. The outcome there could tip the balance and throw the win to one presidential candidate or the other.

## A BUNGLED ELECTION

The state's citizens would not cast a vote for either Adams or Jefferson directly but instead vote for state legislators. Those legislators in turn would choose presidential electors, pledged to support either a Federalist

OPPOSITE: Engraved portrait of Hamilton as Secretary of the Treasury

or a Republican candidate. Since electors had to do as the legislators commanded, in reality the legislature ran the game. The vote there was not proportional—it was a winner-take-all affair, which upped the ante. If Federalists held a majority in the legislature, that body would choose electors pledged to Adams; if Republicans prevailed, Jefferson would be the sole beneficiary. With stakes this high, the 1800 election for New York legislators was slated to be fierce and the contest tight.

Populous New York City was the focus of two savvy political operatives, Republican Aaron Burr and Federalist Alexander Hamilton. Hamilton was a master of policy while Burr, a master tactician, pioneered what is now called a political "ground game." Burr utilized members of New York's Tammany Society, soon to become a political machine in its own right. His team compiled lists of voters, identified characteristics of each, and then dispatched volunteers door-to-door to deliver a customized pitch. For almost two months Burr's home was little more than a campaign headquarters. "Committees were in session day and night during the whole time at his house," according to a New York merchant's diary entry. "Refreshments were always on the table, and mattresses were set up for temporary repose in the rooms. Reports were hourly received from sub-committees—in short, no means left unemployed."[1]

Although he was not nearly as systematic, Hamilton was equally relentless. He continually worked the streets, talking up the Federalist line and "hurrying this way and darting that." His loyal friend Robert Troup campaigned alongside him: "Never have I witnessed such exertions before. I have not eaten dinner for three days and have been constantly on my legs from 7 in the morning till 7 in the afternoon."[2] Competition was intense

OPPOSITE: Trumbull's official vice-presidential portrait of John Adams (c. 1792)

| | Thomas Jefferson of Virginia | Aaron Burr of New York | John Adams of Massachusetts | Charles Cotesworth Pinckney of South Carolina | John Jay of New York |
|---|---|---|---|---|---|
| New Hampshire | | | 6 | 6 | |
| Massachusetts | | | 16 | 16 | |
| Rhode Island | | | 4 | 3 | 1 |
| Connecticut | | | 9 | 9 | |
| Vermont | | | 4 | 4 | |
| New York | 12 | 12 | | | |
| New Jersey | | | 7 | 7 | |
| Pennsylvania | 8 | 8 | 7 | 7 | |
| Delaware | | | 3 | 3 | |
| Maryland | 5 | 5 | 5 | 5 | |
| Virginia | 21 | 21 | | | |
| Kentucky | 4 | 4 | | | |
| North Carolina | 8 | 8 | 4 | 4 | |
| Tennessee | 3 | 3 | | | |
| South Carolina | 8 | 8 | | | |
| Georgia | 4 | 4 | | | |
| | 73 | 73 | 65 | 64 | 1 |

Tally of electoral votes for the 1800 presidential election

but civil. When Hamilton and Burr found themselves working the same crowd, they agreed to take turns.

Votes were cast over a three-day stretch. Eyewitnesses reported that Republicans dispatched "carriages, chairs and wagons" to transport residents to the polls, where Burr and his confederates engaged in a final round of on-the-spot electioneering.[3] In the end, Republicans won all thirteen of the city's priceless allotted seats and thus gained control of the state legislature. To reward Burr for his exertions, national Republican leaders placed him on their ticket. He would be Jefferson's running mate and also provide

regional balance; the Republican ticket would feature both a Southerner and a Northerner.

Panicked, Hamilton attempted to negate the effects of the election by changing the rules midstream. Potentially, the rules could be modified—the Constitution left it up to state legislatures to decide whether to select electors themselves or let voters do it. When Federalists controlled the legislature, Hamilton didn't want voters to be in charge; now, suddenly, he could think of nothing better. He asked his former collaborator John Jay, now serving as New York's governor, to reconvene members of the outgoing Federalist legislature so they could institute popular elections. By now delegates had returned to homes scattered throughout the state, which made the move to reverse the electoral process all the more apparent. Even Hamilton recognized it was blatantly unprincipled. He had willingly abandoned "a strict adherence to ordinary rules" in order to prevent Thomas Jefferson, "an *Atheist* in religion and a *Fanatic* in politics," from becoming president."[4] Jay, to his credit, declined: "Proposing a measure for party purposes . . . would not become me to adopt."[5]

Nobody was surprised that Hamilton would do absolutely anything to prevent Jefferson, a Republican, from becoming president, but all were astonished when he published a vitriolic fifty-four-page assault on Jefferson's opponent, the Federalist John Adams. "There are great and intrinsic defects in his [Adams's] character, which unfit him for the office of Chief Magistrate," he wrote. "He is often liable to paroxysms of anger, which deprive him of self command."[6] Once again Hamilton was attempting to game the system. If he could turn even a few Federalist electors against Adams, South Carolina's Charles Cotesworth Pinckney (Thomas Pinckney's cousin), Adams's running mate and Hamilton's personal pick, would beat him and become president. The scheme came to naught. Adams wound up with sixty-five electoral votes and Pinckney sixty-four. That didn't matter, however, because Jefferson bested them both with seventy-three votes. Strangely, though, Jefferson was not elevated to the presidency either because *his* running mate, Aaron Burr, also had seventy-three votes. Unlike the Federalists, the Republicans displayed perfect party unanimity and *all* voted for both Jefferson and Burr.

According to the Constitution, a tie was to be settled in the House of Representatives with each state delegation casting a single vote. There, Republicans controlled only eight of the sixteen delegations—one shy of the nine votes Jefferson needed to win a majority. In the eyes of the Federalists, Jefferson was a particularly perilous contender. They could deny him the presidency if each and every one of them tossed his vote to Aaron Burr and if they convinced just a few Republican congressmen to do likewise. Even though he was a Republican, a victorious Burr would owe his win to the Federalists.

In this scheme, for once, Hamilton refused to play along. Avowing that Burr was altogether without "public principles," he warned Federalists off. Burr was an opportunist who would "plunder" his country, "disturb our institutions," and seek for himself "permanent power." Much as he had preferred Adams to Jefferson—even though he detested them both—he now argued that Jefferson was "by far not so dangerous a man" as his own longtime antagonist from New York. "For heaven's sake," he pleaded, "let not the Fœderal party be responsible for the elevation of this Man." In Hamilton's circles of hell, Burr inhabited the lowest one.[7]

Nobody listened to Hamilton. The House of Representatives voted thirty-five times in five days, always winding up with a tie. Not until Republican governors of the two largest states, Virginia and Pennsylvania, threatened to mobilize their militias did a handful of Federalists from

OPPOSITE: General Charles Cotesworth Pinckney by James Earl (c. 1795)

key states decide that obstructionist tactics must end before a civil war broke out. On the thirty-sixth ballot, the House of Representatives determined that Thomas Jefferson would be the next president and Aaron Burr vice president.

There is no evidence that Burr supported the Federalists' attempt to make him president, but neither did he withdraw. And of course he could never forget that Hamilton, yet again, had stood in his way.

## CODE DUELLO

That the new democratic republic took thirty-six ballots to determine its president said much about its volatility. As contestants pushed their agendas and jostled for position, they launched vituperative attacks on their opponents. It was a roughhouse world, in which politics was treated as a zero-sum game without rules.

Yet beneath it all was a culture of honor that afforded protection and was understood by any gentleman. In *Affairs of Honor*, the historian Joanne Freeman calls the culture of honor a "source of stability in this contested political landscape," saying it "set standards of conduct and provided a controlled means of handling their violation."[8] Vehement disagreement was permissible, but an attack on honor was deemed out of bounds. If called a scoundrel or liar, a gentleman demanded "satisfaction" by means of an "interview," but the strict *code duello* required that every avenue of escape be exhausted before men actually faced one another, pistols in hand. The principals in the dispute appointed seconds who choreographed a scripted interchange, seeking a mutually acceptable apology. The duel was on if one didn't emerge.

Philip Hamilton, Alexander's oldest son, became embroiled in an affair of honor at the age of nineteen. A recent graduate of Hamilton's own King's College, by then called Columbia, Philip was handsome, intelligent, proud, charming, well-spoken, and drawn to oratory. Something of a paternal replica in all these ways, he inherited another trait: quick to anger, he did not readily retreat.

In a July 4 oration in 1801 before a boisterous crowd, George Eacker, a twenty-seven-year-old fervid Republican, declared that Alexander Hamilton had created an army in order to suppress Republican resistance to Federalist policies; the anticipated invasion by France was only an opportunistic pretext. When the defamatory speech was published, Philip read it, anger building. Much later, on November 20, Philip and his friend Stephen Price spied Eacker at a Manhattan theater performance and entered his box. Verbal sparring led to a public confrontation in a nearby tavern, where Eacker called both his antagonists "rascals," an insult that could not be tolerated. When Eacker refused to retract his remark, Price demanded satisfaction. A mere two days later, on a "field of honor" at Weehawken in New Jersey—duelling was illegal in New York—Price and Eacker fired two shots each. None hit home and both men retired, their reputations secure. They had not died for honor's sake but proved that they were willing to die for it, which was what counted. It was not an unusual outcome.

Philip's reputation, however, was still at issue. John Barker Church, who had returned to New York with

Philip Hamilton, from *The Intimate Life of Alexander Hamilton*, by Allan McLane Hamilton (1910)

Angelica four years before, tried to negotiate a settlement, but Eacker would not withdraw his "rascal" accusation. When Philip's father heard that negotiations had failed, he was distraught. He himself had been a principal to an impending duel eight times, and not one had reached this perilous point.[9] (In 1797 a duel with James Monroe was narrowly averted through the mediation of Aaron Burr.) Philip's life was on the line if he proceeded, but if he did not, he would be dishonored, his reputation in tatters and his future in jeopardy. Conscious of that, Hamilton made no attempt to dissuade him. Instead he advised Philip to reserve his fire until *after* Eacker fired, and then point his pistol to the sky and pull the trigger. The maneuver tempted an adversary to do likewise—or be thought ruthless and, if a shot actually hit home, a murderer.

On the afternoon of the next day, November 23, on the western shore of the Hudson River the ritual commenced. Hamilton and Eacker took ten paces, turned, and stared across the field at each other. The command "Present!" was given. Philip held the expensive, decorated weapon John Church supplied, but it was Eacker who discharged the first round. The bullet entered Philip's body above the hip and toppled him to the ground. Hurriedly he was rowed to New York, brought to the nearby home of Angelica and John Church, and attended by Dr. David Hosack. Alexander Hamilton, a battlefield hero, had fainted on the physician's doorstep after rushing to him for help. Now, Philip lay on a bed between his father and his mother, tossing in pain. Through the night Philip passed in and out of delirium. At five the next morning he died.[10]

Hamilton was inconsolable. When his first-born child was seven months old, he wrote a letter to another of Washington's former aides in which he underscored the attentive, amused affection he gave the infant: "He has a method of waving his hand that announces the future orator. . .

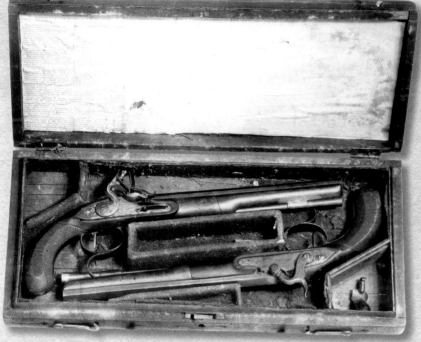

The pistols used in the Hamilton-Burr duel are currently housed in the New York head-quarters of JP Morgan Chase, the bank founded by Burr in 1799.

If he has any fault in manners, he laughs too much."[11] Nine years later, when Philip went away to school, he wrote to him directly. "You remember that I engaged to send for you next Saturday, and I will do it . . . for a promise must never be broken." He then suggested an alternate plan, adding a respectful and loving caveat: "But determine as you like best, and let me know what will be most pleasing to you. A good night to my darling son."[12] Alexander was the father he had never had, but father to this son no longer.

Throngs mourned Philip under falling rain. Hamilton was near collapse and friends held him upright. Eliza was dressed from head to toe in black. She was three months pregnant with her last child—Philip he would be called, as if to will something of the dead son back. There was, of course, no having him back.

# THE GRANGE

Eliza and Alexander grieved. In the first weeks, when they attended a visitor or answered a letter of condolence or sat at the dining table, they felt as if they were only going through the motions. Gradually a sense of reality returned. Perhaps Eliza led the children out to play in newly fallen snow, and its beauty struck her. It was a reprieve from sorrow, God's gift. She chose an embroidery thread for its brilliant color as she listened to John Church recite his lesson. In June she nursed a newborn son. Alexander sought respite on familiar ground, his work. That re-established an order of sorts. He pursued his legal cases and returned to the political fray, writing eighteen essays that attacked President Jefferson's first annual message to Congress. He titled the works "The Examination" and published them in the *New-York Evening Post*, a newspaper that he and some fellow Federalists had inaugurated one week before Philip's death. The first "Examination" installment appeared on December 17, less than four weeks after losing his oldest son.

★ The South Elevation Showing the Thirteen Symbolical Liquidambar Trees at the South-East ★

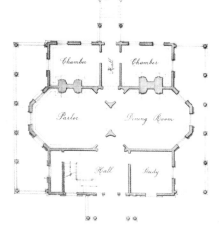

First Floor Plan

★★★ Plan · HAMILTON GRANGE · Elevation ★★★

**OPPOSITE AND ABOVE:** The Grange, as it looked after being built in 1802

★★ *The East Elevation. "The Grange" was begun in 1801 and finished in 1802* ★★

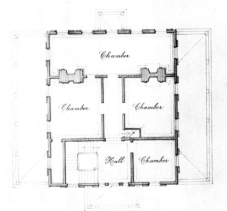

*Second Floor Plan*

★★★    *Plan*    ★ HAMILTON GRANGE ★    *Elevation*    ★★★

**ABOVE:** The Grange's second-floor plan. **OPPOSITE:** A view of the Grange's entrance hall and dining room

Hamilton and his family spent an increasing amount of time at their new home in Harlem Heights, where a few decades earlier retreating militiamen had raced through woods and up narrow bypaths to escape the British. Set on a ridge, it overlooked New York harbor and the city to the south, the Harlem River to the east, and the Hudson River and New Jersey's Palisades to the west. Its commanding views may have been what Hamilton searched for when he surveyed the thirty-two acres in 1800 and began to erect a house. He gave the new estate a name: the Grange. That spoke to a craving. There had been a castle by that name in Scotland, where his forbearers on James Hamilton's side held sway. As a boy, he had passed time on a St. Croix sugar plantation dubbed the Grange, running everywhere while his mother and her sister, Ann, visited. Still weak from the sickness that had carried his mother off, he stood at her grave on that land. The house the Hamiltons constructed was not as grand as either of these edifices, but more than an exhausted, disinherited child had ever had a right to expect. Its title might well have been  a proclamation of the status he claimed in this time and an homage to figures in that long-ago life of his.

More importantly now, the Grange was a refuge. The creation of architect John McComb, who would design City Hall, its interior space was filled with light and air. Two back-to-back octagonal rooms, one a dining room and the other a drawing room, made a single continuous space if the doors were flung open. Bay windows stretched from floor to ceiling; mirrored doors reflected light. An original Gilbert Stuart portrait of Washington, given pride of place, hung on the entryway wall. To the right of the door was a small study, where multifarious books were housed in cabinets with glass doors. Hamilton worked at a roll-top desk but raised his head periodically to gaze out at the meadows and woods or at a

wandering fox. He stopped his pen for a moment to listen to his children race down the overhead hallway that connected the sleeping chambers.

All his life Hamilton freely bestowed love on these children, revealing a domestic, nurturing, and lightly comic side of his nature. A letter written to Eliza from the Grange when she was away in Albany shows this: "I am here, my beloved Betsey, with my two little boys, John and William, who will be my bedfellows tonight. . . . The remainder of the children were well yesterday. Eliza pouts and plays and displays more and more her ample stock of caprice."[13]

John was eleven and William six and Eliza four, and along with the other children, decidedly alive, a solace. Reading the letter, Eliza would think of how he devoted himself to their children. It was a counterweight to the acts of treachery committed in their marriage bed.

If the Grange induced calm and forgiveness, it also brought debt. The purchase price was $55,000 (approximately $1,000,000 in today's

ABOVE: Entrance hall showing the front door to the Grange original sidelights
OPPOSITE: Perspective view of the entrance hall stairs leading to the second floor
FOLLOWING: Hamilton's Grange as it appeared in 1890

dollars), and the Hamiltons dispersed another $25,000 on the construc-tion of the house and improvements to the grounds. There were the usual daily payouts for the cook, servants, and gardener; for firewood that fed multiple, blazing fireplaces; for wines that a stream of houseguests drank down; and for shoes that clad the feet of seven children. As one of the most renowned New York attorneys, Hamilton's income was in the neighbor-hood of $12,000 a year, a substantial sum ordinarily, but no longer. He had to apply himself, his days long. "He lives wholly at his house nine miles from town, so that on an average he must spend three hours a day on the road going and returning between his house and town, which he performs four or five days each week," Rufus King reported.[14] He also scrambled for remuneration—"it will be amazingly convenient to me to touch your money as soon as possible," he wrote a client.[15] In this period everything rested on his shoulders. It was not a good time to duel or to die.

## ALEXANDER HAMILTON V. AARON BURR

What affinity there had once been between Alexander Hamilton and Aaron Burr was by now shattered. In Hamilton's mind Burr was an opportunistic political profligate. In Burr's mind Hamilton was the obstructionist who had blocked his path to both the presidency and, recently, the governorship of New York.

In June of 1804, a grimly vengeful Burr took the obligatory first step toward an "interview." The immediate occasion was a casual reference published by a third party in the *Albany Register*—supposedly, when Burr was running for governor back in February, Hamilton had expressed a "despicable opinion" of him at a political event. This small spark ignited a conflagration. Burr demanded of Hamilton "a prompt and unqualified acknowledgment or denial of the use of any expressions" that could be

AARON BURR

1756    1836

WEEHAWKEN HILL

DRAWN AND ENGRAVED FOR
THE SOCIETY OF ICONOPHILES
NEW YORK 1902

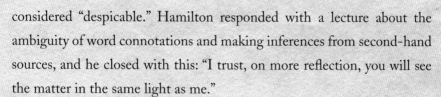
considered "despicable." Hamilton responded with a lecture about the ambiguity of word connotations and making inferences from second-hand sources, and he closed with this: "I trust, on more reflection, you will see the matter in the same light as me."

Resenting such condescension, Burr issued a new demand that Hamilton would find impossible to satisfy: a blanket "retraction or denial" of *anything* he had ever said to "impeach" Burr's character. Although willing to retract a specific inflammatory remark, if it could identified, Hamilton refused to take back all of them when many, he felt, were true and justified.[16]

With neither backing down, Burr and Hamilton prepared for their fateful encounter. Hamilton put his affairs in order in a businesslike manner. He prepared a detailed "Statement on my property and debts," followed by a full explanation of why he had invested so heavily in the Grange. For Eliza's sake, he transferred that property to his brother-in-law, John B. Church, and two others. He left a last will and testament. Appended to the will was a starkly honest account of his quarrel with Burr, which the *New-York Evening Post* made public five days after the duel. In it he wrote, "I have resolved, if our interview is conducted in the usual manner, and it pleases God to give me the opportunity, to *reserve* and *throw away* my first fire, and I have thoughts even of reserving my second fire—and thus giving a double opportunity to Col Burr to pause and to reflect." It was as if once more he was counseling Philip, even though that advice had proved fatal.

And of course he wrote to Eliza. "This letter, my very dear Eliza, will be delivered to you only after my death. If it had been possible for me to have avoided the interview, my love for you and my precious children would have been motive enough. I needn't tell you my pain, not only at leaving you, but in exposing you to the anguish I know you will feel.

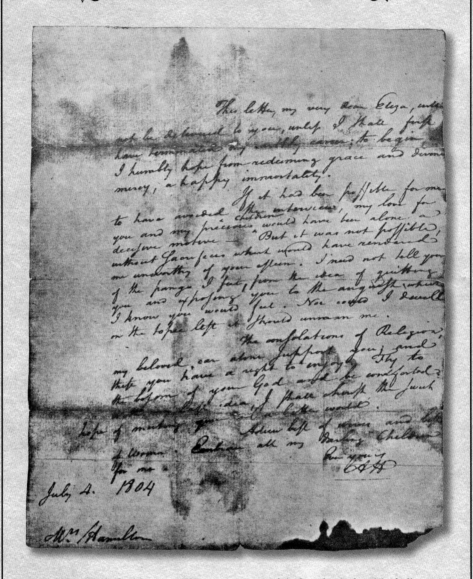

**ABOVE:** Hamilton's final letter to Eliza, written a week before the duel and including instructions only to be delivered if "I shall first have terminated my earthly career" **OPPOSITE:** A page from Hamilton's statement of property and debts which he wrote out prior to the duel with Burr

they would this summer and fall reach the point,
at which it is my intention they should stop,
at least 'till I should be better able than at
present to add to them; and ~~upon~~ after a
fair examination founded upon an actual account
of my expenditures, I am persuaded that a
plan I have contemplated for the next and
succeeding years would bring my expences of
every kind within the compass of four thousand
Dollars yearly, exclusive of the interest of my
country establishment. To this limit, I have
been resolved to reduce them, even though it should
be necessary to leave that establishment for
a few years.

      In the mean time, my
Settlement
lands now on a count of Sale would accelerate
the extinguishment of my debt, and in
the end leave me a handsome clear property
It was also allowable for me to take into
view, collaterally, the expectations of my
wife; which have been of late partly realized
She is now intitled to ~~an~~ a property of between
two ~~and~~ three thousand pounds (as I compute
by descent from her mother; and her father
" understood to possess a large estate. I feel
all the delicacy of this allusion; but the occasion
I trust will plead my excuse. And that
venerable father, I am sure, will pardon — He
knows well all the nicety of my past conduct

      Viewing the matter in these
different aspects, I trust the opinion of candid
men will be, that there has been no impropriety in my conduct; especially when it
is taken into the ~~a~~ calculation that my
establishment, though costly, promises, by
Country
the progressive rise of property on this
Island, and the felicity of its situation
to become more and more valuable —

I cannot dwell on this topic or it will unman me."[17] That was one week before the interview, and the message, however painful, was succinct and clear. His final letter, written "Tuesday Evening 10 oCL," the eve of the scheduled "interview," was almost in different hand, several words barely decipherable:

> The scruples of a Christian have determined me to expose my own life to any extent rather than subject myself to the guilt of taking the life of another. This must increase my hazards and redoubles my pangs for you. But you had rather I should die innocent than live guilty. Heaven can preserve me and I humbly hope will; but, in the contrary event, I charge you to remember that you are a Christian. God's Will be done! The will of a merciful God must be good. Once more Adieu My Darling darling Wife, AH[18]

**ABOVE:** William Van Ness served as Aaron Burr's second in Burr's duel with Alexander Hamilton.
**RIGHT:** Dr. David Hosack was the physician who attended to both Philip and Alexander Hamilton during their ill-fated duels.

ABOVE: Hamilton (right) and Burr prepare for their duel. FOLLOWING: A bucolic view of the duel site as it once looked.

At first light on Wednesday, July 11, 1804, Hamilton and his second, Nathaniel Pendleton; Burr and his second, William Van Ness; and David Hosack, the physician who had attended to Philip Hamilton, arrived at a small, secluded flat by the Hudson River in Weehawken, New Jersey. Hamilton gripped the same ornate pistol Philip had held. He and Burr both discharged one shot each. Who did so first has been eternally debated, along with the intentions of the two—what part was premeditation, what part accident, what part an attempt to throw a shot away. The only uncontested fact is that the ball fired by Burr hit Hamilton's hip; from there it seems to have ricocheted into his abdomen, piercing his liver, diaphragm, and lumbar vertebra. Dr. Hosack attended him. "This is a mortal wound, Doctor," Hamilton told him.[19]

Hamilton was lifted into a boat and rowed back across the Hudson, almost lifeless. From the landing dock he was carried to the adjoining mansion of William Bayard, a friend. There he was laid on a bed, dosed with a tincture of opium, and stripped of his blood-soaked clothing. When Eliza arrived from the Grange, she fanned his fevered face, alarmed but believing what she was first told, that it was "spasms—no one dared tell her the truth."[20]

Hamilton still spoke clearly. In the afternoon he received the last sacrament. The next day others came, some falling to their knees in prayer.

Hamilton was well aware of the seriousness of the wound.

The mansion of William Bayard, director of the Bank of New York, where Hamilton died

Angelica was with Eliza as the strength drained from her husband, both grieving. It was now a deathwatch. Briefly the children appeared, placed in a row at the foot of the bed so Hamilton could see them all together. Early that afternoon he perished.

# Epilogue

## Family Loyalty

ALEXANDER HAMILTON'S CLOSE FRIEND JAMES MCHENRY ONCE TOLD him that Eliza Hamilton had "as much merit as your treasurer as you have as treasurer of the wealth of the United States."[1] She was capable and did oversee the management of the household, especially during Hamilton's long absences. But there was no way that she could manage the $60,000 debt that landed in her lap after his death. When Philip Schuyler died three months later, there wasn't much left of his estate to pass on to her. Betsey was mother to seven children, including a two-year-old, three older boys who required an education, and one (her oldest child, Angelica) who suffered from mental illness.

Eliza had no choice. The Grange had to be sold. It was then that Hamilton's executors stepped forward, men who were also his longtime partners and friends. Rescuing Eliza, they bought the house and property

OPPOSITE: Engraved portrait of Hamilton by William G. Jackman

and then sold it back to her for half of what they had paid. Gouverneur Morris raised funds for her support through a subscription. Even so, without a husband's steady income, her finances vacillated and she struggled. She applied for Hamilton's veteran's benefits. Sometimes she took small loans.

Eliza lived on as a widow for fifty-five years. She was sustained by religion and a restless, fix-it temperament that was akin to Hamilton's but rooted in compassion for others, especially the young. Alongside like-minded allies, she founded the New York Orphan Asylum Society. For decades she organized, raised funds, and fought to make sure that the asylum's furnace had ample coal or children had shoes or a promising boy attended a military academy. She inaugurated the Hamilton Free School, in Washington Heights, on land that she had donated. It was in Eliza's nature to do what she could when she could and see it through from start to finish, attending to every detail.

But Betsey's principal project through the years was Alexander Hamilton himself, much as he had been when alive. Dressed in stiff, black dresses that declared her a widow, she remained constant and indomitable to his memory. She had in mind a biography, monumental in scope, which would edify admirers and constrain detractors. She sought out papers and wrote those who knew him, quizzing them and eliciting answers—"Your early acquaintance with my husband—when, and the circumstances of it? His appearance and manners then?"[2]

Not all of what Hamilton had written came easily to hand. Eliza vividly recalled his working on President Washington's acclaimed Farewell Address—"The whole or nearly all the 'Address,' was read to me by him as he wrote it and a greater part if not all was written by him in my presence."[3] The draft was not among the papers she unearthed. When

Friends & Fellow Citizens

The period for a new election of a Citizen, to administer the Executive government of the United States, being not far distant, and the time actually arrived, when your thoughts must be employed in designating the person, who is to be cloathed with that important trust for an ~~instance~~, it appears to me proper, especially as it may conduce to a more distinct expression of the public voice, that I should now apprise you of the resolution I have formed, to decline being considered among the number of those, out of whom a choice is to be made. —

I beg you, at the same time, to do me the justice to be assured, that this resolution has not been taken, without a strict regard to all the considerations appertaining to the relation, which binds a dutiful citizen to his country — and that, in withdrawing the tender of service which silence in my situation might imply, I am influenced by no diminution of ~~zeal~~ for your future interest, no deficiency ~~of~~ grateful respect for your past kindness; but ~~am~~ ~~supported~~ by a ~~full~~ convictio

OPPOSITE: This gold mourning ring with a central mount framing a braid of Hamilton's hair was given as a gift to one of his friends by Eliza in 1805. ABOVE: Washington's Farewell Address, which Hamilton had helped him craft

she discovered it was in the possession of Rufus King, one of Hamilton's political allies, she dispatched her son James Alexander to fetch it. King refused to give it up. Since Americans believed that Washington wrote the address himself, King judged that "public opinion, upon this subject, should not be disturbed." John Church, James's younger brother, visited King's residence next and, by King's account, "thought himself at liberty to menace me in my own house."[4] King still held firm. He only relented when Eliza filed suit. At last she received her long-sought-after proof—the Farewell Address in Hamilton's script, together with Washington's comments on it in his hand.

Eliza hired assistant after assistant to search through thousands of her husband's papers and biographer after biographer to make something of the massive portfolio. Hamilton was not easy to digest. Biographers gave it up or passed away. The work in the end fell to John Church Hamilton, who had yet to turn twelve when his father was killed by Aaron Burr. From the early-1830s to the mid-1860s, John's life was subsumed by the project. A two-volume biography, published in 1834, was followed in 1850 by *The Works of Alexander Hamilton* in seven volumes.

Eliza was ninety-three by this time and no doubt relieved to see her project come to fruition. Four years later she was on her deathbed, her son James sitting by. Speaking clearly, she asked him to rearrange her bedclothes. When he did, her eyes closed. Minutes later, he put a finger on her wrist to feel for a pulse and there was none.

Alfred T. Agate portrait of John Church Hamilton

John Church Hamilton toiled on, Eliza's vision fully his own by now. In 1856, he released the first of another seven-volume series, this one titled *History of the Republic of the United States of America, as Traced in the Writings of Alexander Hamilton and of his Contemporaries.* In this tome, Hamilton was the protagonist, at the hub of the nation's history. His political opponents were the tale's antagonists, no more than Hamilton's foils. The narrative was sometimes sound, sourced from contemporaneous documentation. At points, though, this tribute to his father was drawn from folkloric chronicles or deliberately embellished. Nevertheless, John's account took hold, with biographers and historians drawing from it repeatedly and liberally.

## The Rap On Hamilton

Alexander Hamilton and Thomas Jefferson are long dead, but the debates they triggered live on. Lining up behind one figurehead or the other, historians have divided into camps. Comparing the two founders, one recent author, Darren Staloff, views Jefferson as a Romantic and Hamilton as decidedly ahead of his time:

> Hamilton's program was the most modern and progressive of the founding era. Ever the champion of commercial interests, he promoted rapid industrialization and urban growth fostered by a strong central government capable of projecting its interests and its power in the world at large.... No other founding father or leader of the early republic grasped as clearly and embraced as unflinchingly the modern world we have inherited. To that extent at least, as modern Americans in the most powerful country on earth, we are all the children of Alexander Hamilton.[5]

For their part, Jeffersonians set Hamilton's accomplishments aside and cast him as cold, calculating, and authoritarian. "There is nothing in him to appeal to our democratic instincts," Walt Whitman once wrote, and Franklin Delano Roosevelt lamented his "contempt for the opinion of the masses."[6] It's even been said that Hamilton referred to the people, collectively, as "a great beast." The accusation appeared fifty-five years after Hamilton's death in a fourth-hand reminiscence and was popularized by Henry Adams, a great-great-grandson of Hamilton's arch-enemy John Adams. As questionable as the allegation is, it's often repeated.[7]

Leading Jefferson scholars have particularly demonized Hamilton, their hero's bête noire. Dumas Malone, whose mid-twentieth century six-volume biography of Jefferson was considered definitive for decades, declaimed that Hamilton's "contempt for the stupidity of the lesser orders of mankind" would have led "straight to Fascism." Merrill Peterson, another prominent Jefferson biographer, said that Hamilton's ideas were "more European than American" and claimed his commitment was "not to America but to his own glorious image of a great nation." Julian Boyd, noted editor of *The Papers of Thomas Jefferson*, wrote a seventy-eight page diatribe on Hamilton that he inappropriately inserted in volume 18 of the Jefferson papers themselves. Hamilton, Boyd claimed, fabricated the alleged affair with Maria Reynolds to cover up financial wrongdoing and was, as suspected, entirely corrupt. He "took his guidance from the old order, Jefferson from the new."[8]

It's easy to see why Jefferson, the supposed proponent of individual freedom, self-sufficiency, and small government, has historically outpolled Hamilton and his big banks. On the Fourth of July, Americans shoot off fireworks to celebrate our liberty, not our monetary policies, robust central government, economic stability, manufacturing prowess, or concentration of capital. True, Jefferson's personal reputation has been called into question

*Mrs. Alexander Hamilton* (1825)

recently—there are his slaves to consider and a likely affair with one, Sally Hemings. But the ideals he espoused are always popular, while inside deal-making, Hamilton's domain, is ever suspect.

In 1943, on Jefferson's two-hundredth birthday, his great admirer, President Roosevelt, dedicated the Thomas Jefferson Memorial in Washington, D.C. The bicentennial of Hamilton's birth came the following decade, but no memorial in the nation's capital was forthcoming. When Congress's Alexander Hamilton Bicentennial Commission tried to interest movie producers in making a film about him, it found no takers.[9]

The Grange as it looked while being moved, 1889

Each year close to half-a-million historical pilgrims visit Jefferson's carefully conserved home, Monticello, which is set on plantation lands with magnificent vistas. In contrast, the Grange land was subdivided into 300 lots in the 1880s and the house relocated a block to the south, its view entirely erased. By 1960 the *New York Times* reported that it was "hardly noticed by the public. Plaster falls from its ceilings, paint peels from its walls, and small boys delight in breaking its windows."[10]

Two years later a bill designating Hamilton's Grange a national monument was attached to a constitutional amendment that outlawed poll taxes, which discouraged African Americans from voting. For nine days senators from the South staged a filibuster, but in the end the conjoined measures passed. Befittingly, the only home that Hamilton ever owned was preserved through political finagling—but, importantly, it was preserved. That was in 1962, and before long the Grange's first visitors passed through its doors. But three decades later, in another reversal, the National Park Service closed it down because it was structurally unsound and a hazard.

# HAMILTON IN RAP

A founder's popularity waxes and wanes depending on the circumstances, and a recent shift in perspective has improved Hamilton's ratings. In blockbuster biographies that appeared one after the other in the last two decades, founders were no longer "larger than life, giants in the earth," as historian Gordon Wood noted.[11] Each one had "his flaws and failing," added David McCullough, the biographer of John Adams.[12] Joseph Ellis, the author of *Founding Brothers*, spoke of "their mutual imperfections and fallibilities, as well as their eccentricities and excesses."[13] In such writings founders were not so much reduced as made human. No one argued the fact that they gave us much—a country. At the same time they were recognizably like us, which, oddly, only increased their attraction.

On this newly leveled playing field, Hamilton could possibly be seen as just one more flesh-and-blood player, not the odd man out. In his 2004 biography *Alexander Hamilton*, the historian Ron Chernow interpreted the man for our own time. His subject was error-prone but sympathetic; he had shortcomings but made indisputable contributions. "To repudiate his legacy is, in many ways, to repudiate the modern world," Chernow asserted.[14]

Four years after Chernow's bestseller appeared, the Grange was moved again, this time to Nicholas Park, where it was once more surrounded by trees and lawns. It also underwent an extensive restoration. An estimated $14 million later, Alexander and Eliza would have been able to walk through the door and recognize the home they had built two centuries before.

Hamilton was already on an upswing by the time a smash-hit Broadway musical catapulted him to new heights in 2015. *Hamilton*, the

**FOLLOWING:** A statue of Hamilton at his namesake college in Clinton, New York

show, was the brainchild of electrifying playwright, composer, and actor Lin-Manuel Miranda, whose parents arrived as immigrants from their own Caribbean island, Puerto Rico. Miranda read Chernow's 731-page *Hamilton* while on vacation in Mexico. Inspired, he obtained the theatrical rights to the book and generated his own take on a Hamilton who tells his story in modern-day hip-hop rhyme. Without lineage or fortune, this newcomer advances against all the odds. He is as unstoppable as the pulsating music and exuberant dancing.

A question appears at the conclusion of Miranda's *Hamilton*: "Who lives, who dies, who tells the story?" In history that is the question to ask. Hamilton's family and Hamiltonians have had their turn. In their telling, Alexander Hamilton is an unabashed hero. As Jeffersonians tell it, Hamilton hungers after power. Chernow's biography rescued Hamilton from "cynical misappropriation," as one critic says, while Lin-Manuel Miranda reinvented his narrative for a new age.

Miranda has tapped into a demographic of immigrants, minorities, millennials, and youngsters—including the thousands of students who view the play gratis each year and countless more who listen to and sing its score. These diverse Americans see Hamilton as their own founding father. Through drive and talent, he rose up and gained a seat at the table "in the room where it happened," to cite Miranda. Often condemned as elitist, Hamilton delivers hope to other outsiders now. If Alexander Hamilton could make a difference, so can they. His rise is America's story, but it took the nation more than two centuries to see it that way.

# Further Reading

## Primary Sources

Farrand, Max. *The Records of the Federal Convention of 1787* (1911). Three volumes. Includes the notes taken by James Madison and others at the Constitutional Convention. To access this online, search for "Farrand's Records" and choose either the "memory.loc.gov" URL or the "oll.libertyfund.org" URL.

*The Federalist Papers* (originally titled *The Federalist: A Collection of Essays, Written in Favour of the New Constitution*). Numerous editions are available, in print or online.

Hamilton, Alexander. *Papers of Alexander Hamilton*, Harold C. Syrett and Jacob E. Cooke, eds. (New York: Columbia University Press, 1961–1987). This collection is essential to any serious study of Hamilton, and the comprehensive editorial comments provide invaluable context. In our reference notes, we abbreviate this source as *PAH*.

Jensen, Merrill, et al, eds. *Documentary History of the Ratification of the Constitution* (Madison: State Historical Society of Wisconsin, 1976—). Twenty-seven volumes are completed, with five more still to come. Includes *The Federalist* essays and the circumstances of their publication.

National Archives, *Founders Online: http://founders.archives.gov/*. This site provides online access to the Hamilton Papers, which is a tremendous asset. Navigation is problematic, however. If you are trying to pin down a direct quotation, enter several words into your search engine, within quotation marks. Then click the URL "founders.archives.gov" from the selections that emerge. Otherwise, on-site, you can browse chronologically, narrowing the search by entering author, recipient, or date if you have that information.

## Writings and Recollections by Family and Friends

Baxter, Katherine Schuyler. *A Godchild of Washington* (London and New York, F. Tennyson Neely, 1897).

Hamilton, Allan McLane. *The Intimate Life of Alexander Hamilton* (New York: Charles Scribner's Sons, 1910).

Hamilton, James A. *Reminiscences* (New York: Charles Scribner, 1869).

Hamilton, John Church. *A History of the Republic of the United States of America: As Traced in the Writings of Alexander Hamilton and of his Contemporaries* (Philadelphia: J. B. Lippincott, 1857–1864).

Humphreys, Mary Gay. *Catherine Schuyler* (New York: Charles Scribner's Sons, 1897).

Schachner, Nathan. "Alexander Hamilton Viewed by His Friends: The Narratives of Robert Troup and Hercules Mulligan," *William and Mary Quarterly,* Third Series, 4:2 (April, 1947), 203–225.

## Biographies

Of the abundance of biographies, both past and present, these deserve special note:

Chernow, Ron. *Alexander Hamilton* (New York: Penguin, 2004). This is the well-researched and highly entertaining book that inspired Lin-Manuel Miranda's musical *Hamilton.* It's is a must-read for those who want a detailed (730 pages) biography.

Mitchell, Broadus. *Alexander Hamilton: Youth to Maturity, 1755–1788* (New York: Macmillan, 1962). For decades, this six-volume tome was the go-to biography for all things Hamilton.

Newton, Michael E. *Alexander Hamilton, The Formative Years* (Eleftheria Publishing, 2015). A must for Hamilton buffs, but not casual readers. Newton dissects primary sources like no previous author.

Wilser, Jeff. *Alexander Hamilton's Guide to Life* (New York: Three Rivers Press, 2016). This bright and witty work *is* for casual readers, but Hamilton buffs beware—the old tales appear, whether based on evidence or rumor.

## Aaron Burr and his Duel with Hamilton

Brands, H. W. *The Heartbreak of Aaron Burr* (New York: Anchor, 2012).

Ellis, Joseph. *Founding Brothers: The Revolutionary Generation* (New York: Alfred A. Knopf, 2001). The first chapter covers the duel.

Fleming, Thomas. *Duel: Alexander Hamilton, Aaron Burr, and the Future of America* (New York: Basic Books, 1999).

Isenberg, Nancy. *Fallen Founder, The Life of Aaron Burr* (New York, New York: Penguin Books, 2007).

Rogow, Arnold. *A Fatal Friendship: Alexander Hamilton and Aaron Burr* (New York: Hill and Wang, 1999).

Sedgwick, John. *War of Two: Alexander Hamilton, Aaron Burr, and the Duel that Stunned the Nation* (New York: Berkley Books, 2015).

## Other Joint Biographies

Ferling, John. *Jefferson and Hamilton: The Rivalry that Forged a Nation* (New York: Bloomsbury Press, 2013).

Kennedy, Roger. *Burr, Hamilton, and Jefferson: A Study in Character* (New York: Oxford University Press, 2000).

Knott Stephen F. and Tony Williams. *Washington and Hamilton: The Alliance that Forged America* (Naperville, IL: Sourcebooks, 2016).

Staloff, Darren. *Hamilton, Adams, Jefferson: The Politics of Enlightenment and the American Founding* (New York: Hill and Wang, 2005).

## Hamilton's Legacy
Knott, Stephen F. *Alexander Hamilton and the Persistence of Myth* (Lawrence, KS: University of Kansas Press, 2002).

## Backgrounds
Burrows, Edwin G. and Mike Wallace. *Gotham: A History of New York City to 1898* (New York: Oxford University Press, 1999). All you would ever want to know about New York City in Hamilton's day, or for any day prior to the Twentieth Century.

Klarman, Michael J. *The Framers' Coup: The Making of the United States Constitution* (New York: Oxford University Press, 2016.) A comprehensive historical synthesis, from the turbulent Confederation to the Bill of Rights.

Martin, Joseph Plumb. *Private Yankee Doodle: Being A Narrative of Some of the Adventures, Dangers and Sufferings of a Revolutionary* (Boston: Little, Brown & Co., 1962; first published in 1830 under the title *A narrative of some of the adventures, dangers, and sufferings of a Revolutionary soldier, interspersed with anecdotes of incidents that occurred within his own observation*). The most entertaining firsthand account of life in the Continental Army you will ever find.

Raphael, Ray. *Constitutional Myths: What We Get Wrong and How to Get It Right* (New York: The New Press, 2013). Traces Hamilton's evolving positions at the Constitutional Convention, in *The Federalist* essays, and as Secretary of the Treasury.

Raphael, Ray. *Mr. President: How and Why the Framers Created a Chief Executive* (New York: Alfred A. Knopf, 2012). Covers Hamilton's role in creating and implementing a strong presidency.

Sharp, James Roger. *American Politics in the Early Republic: The New Nation in Crisis* (New Haven: Yale University Press, 1993). A survey of the complex politics of the 1790s.

Stuart, Andrea. *Sugar in the Blood* (New York: Alfred A. Knopf, 2013). The Caribbean Islands in colonial times.

# Endnotes

1 The principal primary source is *The Papers of Alexander Hamilton*, eds. Harold C. Syrett and Jacob E. Cooke (New York: Columbia University Press, 1961–1987). After the first reference, this will be abbreviated as *PAH*.

## CHAPTER 1: THE SUGAR ISLANDS

1 Eric Williams, *Capitalism and Slavery* (Chapel Hill: University of North Carolina Press, 1944, 1994), 53.

2 John Adams to Benjamin Rush, 25 January 1806, Founder Online, National Archives, https://founders.archives.gov/?q=Project%3A%22Adams%20Papers%22%20Author%3A%22Adams%2C%20John%22%20Recipient%3A%22Rush%2C%20Benjamin%22&s=1511311111&r=34 An alternate transcription is "bastard brat of a Scotch Pedler."

3 Michael E. Newton, *Alexander Hamilton: The Formative Years* (Eleftheria Publishing, 2015), 14.

4 AH to William Jackson, 26 August 1800, *The Papers of Alexander Hamilton*, eds. Harold C. Syrett and Jacob E. Cooke (New York: Columbia University Press, 1961–1987) 25:88–91. Henceforth this source will be abbreviated as *PAH*.

5 Newton, *Alexander Hamilton*, 15.

6 Newton, *Alexander Hamilton*, 16; Ron Chernow, *Alexander Hamilton* (New York: Penguin, 2004), 13.

7 Edwin G. Burrows and Mike Wallace, *Gotham: A History of New York City to 1898* (New York: Oxford University Press, 1999), 120.

8 Chernow, *Alexander Hamilton*, 19.

9 Andrea Stuart, *Sugar in the Blood* (New York: Alfred A. Knopf, 2013), 163.

10 P. J. Marshall, *The Oxford History of the British Empire: The Eighteenth Century* (Oxford: Oxford University Press, 1998), 396–97.

11 AH to William Hamilton, 2 May 1797, *PAH* 21:77.

12 *PAH* 1:8.

13 AH to Edward Stevens, 11 November 1769, *PAH* 1:4.

14 *Published in the Royal Danish American Gazette*, 6 September, 1772, *PAH* 1:34–38.

## CHAPTER 2: AN IMMIGRANT RISES

1 AH to Edward Stevens, 11 November 1769, *PAH* 1:4.

2 Gouverneur Morris to John Penn, 20 May 1774, *American Archives*, Fourth Series, ed. Peter Force (New York: Johnson Reprint Company, 1972; first published 1833–1846), 1:342–343.

3 Nathan Schachner, "Alexander Hamilton Viewed by His Friends: The Narratives of Robert Troup and Hercules Mulligan," *William and Mary Quarterly*, Third Series, 4:2 (April 1947): 209.

4 Schachner, "Narratives of Troup and Mulligan," 211.

5 Burrows and Wallace, *Gotham*, 120.

6 Ray Raphael and Marie Raphael, *The Spirit of '74: How the American Revolution Began* (New York: The New Press, 2015), 22.

7 Raphael and Raphael, *The Spirit of '74*, 28.

8 Editor's note, *PAH* 1:43.

**OPPOSITE:** Sculptor James Earle Fraser created this statue of Hamilton, which stands in front of the southern facade of the Treasury Building in Washington D.C.

9  *Journals of the Continental Congress*, 20 October 1774, 1:75–80, Library of Congress, American Memory, A Century of Lawmaking for the New Nation, http://memory.loc.gov/cgi-bin/query/r?ammem/hlaw:@field(DOCID+@lit(jc00137)

10  *PAH* 1:45.

11  *PAH* 1:45–165.

12  Schachner, "Narratives of Troup and Mulligan," 214.

13  *PAH* 1:167.

14  Schachner, "Narratives of Troup and Mulligan," 211.

15  AH to John Jay, 26 November 1775, *PAH* 1:176–77.

16  AH to Edward Stevens, 11 November 1769, *PAH* 1:4.

17  Schachner, "Narratives of Troup and Mulligan," 210.

18  Newton, *Alexander Hamilton*, 143.

19  Burrows and Wallace, *Gotham*, 240.

20  Thomas Paine, "The American Crisis, Number 1," *Thomas Paine: Collected Writings*, ed. Eric Foner (New York: Library of America, 1995), 91.

21  Henry Knox to Lucy Knox, 28 December 1776, Newton, *Alexander Hamilton*, 180.

22  George Washington to James McHenry, 29 July 1798, *Papers of George Washington*, Retirement Series, ed. W. W. Abbot (Charlottesville: University of Virginia Press, 1998), 2:472–74.

23  Ibid.

24  Washington to Joseph Reed, 23 January 1776, *Papers of George Washington*, Revolutionary War Series, 3:172–175.

25  Chernow, *Alexander Hamilton*, 91.

26  Benjamin Rush to Thomas Ruston, 19 October 1775, in *The Founders on the Founders: Word Portraits from the American Revolutionary Era*, ed. John Kaminski

(Charlottesville: University of Virginia Press, 2008), 474.

27  Elizabeth Dyer to Joseph Trumbull, Philadelphia, 15 June 1775, in *The Founders on the Founders*, 471.

28  John Laurens to Henry Laurens, 26 October 1776, in David Duncan Wallace, *The Life of Henry Laurens* (New York: G. P. Putnam's Sons, 1915), 447.

29  AH to Jay, 14 March 1779, in *PAH* 2:17–19.

30  James R. Gaines, *For Liberty and Glory: Washington, Lafayette, and Their Revolutions* (New York: W. W. Norton, 2007), 37.

31  Katherine Schuyler Baxter, *A Godchild of Washington* (London and New York: F. Tennyson Neely, 1897), 225.

32  AH to John Laurens, 22 May 1779, *PAH* 2:53–54.

**CHAPTER 3: THE PERILS OF WAR**

1   AH to Hugh Knox, 17 June 1777, *PAH* 26:360.

2   David Hackett Fischer, *Washington's Crossing* (New York: Oxford University Press, 2002), 358.

3   AH to Gouverneur Morris, 1 September 1777, *PAH* 1:321.

4   Charles Royster, *A Revolutionary People at War: The Continental Army and American Character, 1775–1783* (Chapel Hill: University of North Carolina Press, 1979), 225.

5   In Marc Leepson, *Lafayette: Lessons in Leadership from the Idealistic General* (New York: Palgrave Macmillan, 2011), 37.

6   Henry Laurens to John Lewis Gervais, 8 October 1777, *The Papers of Henry Laurens*, ed. Philip M. Hamer (Columbia: University of South Carolina Press, 1968-2003), 11:547.

7   AH to John Hancock, 18 September 1777, *PAH* 1:326.

8   Newton, *Alexander Hamilton*, 251.

9   George Washington to AH, 30 October 1777, *PAH* 1:347.

10 Chernow, *Alexander Hamilton*, 102.

11 John Fitzgerald to Washington, enclosure in letter, 16 February 1778, in Newton, *Alexander Hamilton*, 265.

12 Washington to Thomas Conway, 5 November 1777, *Papers of George Washington*, Revolutionary War Series, 12:129–130.

13 AH to George Clinton, 13 February 1778, *PAH* 1:428.

14 Newton, *Alexander Hamilton*, 282.

15 Joseph Plumb Martin, *Private Yankee Doodle: Being a Narrative of Some of the Adventures, Dangers and Sufferings of a Revolutionary*, ed. George F. Scheer (Boston: Little, Brown & Co., 1962), 127, 131.

16 AH to Elias Boudinot, 5 July 1778, *PAH* 1:512.

17 John Laurens to Henry Laurens, 30 June 1778, *Papers of Henry Laurens*, 13:532–537.

18 AH to Boudinot, 5 July 1778, *PAH* 1:510–511.

19 Newton, *Alexander Hamilton*, 291.

20 Charles Lee to Washington, 30 June 1778, *Papers of George Washington*, Revolutionary War Series, 15: 594–595.

21 Washington to Lee, 30 June 1778, 15:595–596.

22 Statement of Hamilton and Evan Edwards, 24 December 1778, *PAH* 1:604.

23 Joseph Lee Boyle, "Weather and the Continental Army," on file at Valley Forge National Historical Park.

24 Joseph Plumb Martin, *Private Yankee Doodle*, 172.

25 Joseph Plumb Martin, *Private Yankee Doodle*, 182.

26 AH to James Duane, 3 September 1780, *PAH* 2:406, 416–417.

## CHAPTER 4: THE POWER OF LOVE

1 AH to John Laurens, April 1779, *PAH* 2:37.

2 Letters from Eric Olson's "Dancing in Morristown" file, Morristown National Historical Park.

3 Philip Schuyler to AH, 8 April 1780, *PAH* 2:305–306.

4 AH to Elizabeth Schuyler, 5 October 1780, *PAH* 2:455–456.

5 In Robert Hendrickson, *The Rise and Fall of Alexander Hamilton* (New York: Van Nostrand Reinhold, 1985), 427.

6 AH to Philip Schuyler, February 18, 1781, *PAH* 2:563–568.

7 Ibid.

8 General Lafayette to George Washington, 24 May 1781, *Correspondence and Manuscripts of General Lafayette* (London: n.p., 1838), 417.

9 Lafayette to AH, 23 May 1781, *PAH* 2:643–645.

10 AH to Elizabeth Hamilton, 10 July 1781, *PAH* 2:647.

11 Broadus Mitchell, *Alexander Hamilton: Youth to Maturity, 1755–1788* (New York: Macmillan, 1962), 251.

12 Ronald Blumer, *American Experience: Alexander Hamilton*, PBS documentary (St. Paul: Twin Cities Public Television 2007). Transcript: http://www.pbs.org/wgbh/amex/hamilton/filmmore/pt.html

13 AH to Lafayette, 15 October 1781, *PAH* 2:681.

14 Newton, *Alexander Hamilton*, 498.

15 AH to Elizabeth Hamilton, 16 October 1782, *PAH* 2:682

16 AH to John Laurens, 15 August 1782, *PAH* 3:145.

17 AH to Laurens, 30 March 1780, *PAH* 2:303–304.

## CHAPTER 5: MODEL CITIZEN

1 Alexander McDougall to Philip Schuyler, 12 October 1781, in Chernow, *Alexander Hamilton*, 169.

2 Mary Gay Humphreys, *Catherine Schuyler* (New York: Charles Scribner's Sons, 1897), 198.

3 AH to James Duane, 3 September 1780, *PAH* 2:404.

4   AH to Robert Morris, 30 April 1781, *PAH* 2:606.

5   Editorial note, *PAH* 2:604.

6   Morris to Benjamin Harrison, 15 January 1782, *The Papers of Robert Morris*, ed. E. James Ferguson (Pittsburg: University of Pittsburg Press, 1973), 4:46.

7   AH to Elizabeth Hamilton, 22 July 1783, *PAH* 3:413.

8   AH to Robert R. Livingston, 13 August 1783, *PAH* 3:431.

9   AH to Lafayette, 3 November 1782, *PAH* 3:192.

10  "A Letter from Phocian to the Considerate Citizens of New York," *PAH* 3:483–84.

11  Chernow, *Alexander Hamilton*, 210.

12  *PAH* 3:597.

13  *PAH* 3:514–18.

14  AH to Morris, 13 August 1782, *PAH* 3:137–138.

15  AH to John Steele, 15 October 1792, *PAH* 12:568.

16  John P. Kaminski, *George Clinton: Yeoman Politician of the New Republic* (Madison, WI: Madison House Publishers, 1993), 277.

17  *PAH* 20:281.

18  Clarence Ver Steeg, *Robert Morris: Revolutionary Financier* (New York: Octagon Books, 1972), 166–167.

## CHAPTER 6: ENVISIONING A NATION

1   AH to James Duane, 3 September 1780, *PAH* 2:400–418.

2   "Continental Congress Unsubmitted Resolution Calling for a Convention to Amend the Articles of Confederation," *PAH* 3:420–426.

3   AH to William Hamilton, 2 May 1797, *PAH* 27:77–78.

4   John Church Hamilton, *A History of the Republic of the United States of America: As Traced in the Writings of Alexander Hamilton and of His Contemporaries* (Philadelphia: J. B. Lippincott, 1868), 3:161.

5   AH to Richard Varick, 1 September 1786, *PAH* 3:683.

6   AH, under the pseudonym "H. G.," in *The Daily Advertiser* (New York), 4 March 1789, *PAH* 5:288.

7   George Washington to Thomas Jefferson, 30 May 30, 1787, *The Papers of Thomas Jefferson*, ed. Julian P. Boyd (Princeton, NJ: Princeton University Press, 1955), 11:391.

8   Max Farrand, *The Records of the Federal Convention of 1787* (New Haven: Yale University Press, 1966), vol. 3, appendix B http://oll.libertyfund.org/titles/farrand-the-records-of-the-federal-convention-of-1787-vol-3.

9   Hamilton's outline of his plan, the notes he jotted down in preparation for the speech, and renditions of the speech recorded by delegates James Madison, Robert Yates, John Lansing Jr., and Rufus King are in *PAH* 4:178–211, and in Farrand, *Records of the Federal Convention*, vol. 3, appendix F.

10  This is from Robert Yates's notes in Farrand, *Records of the Federal Convention*.

11  William Pierce, "Character Sketches of Delegates to the Constitutional Convention," in Farrand, *Records of the Federal Convention*, 3:89.

12  *PAH* 4:178.

13  AH to Washington, 3 July 1787, *PAH* 4:224.

14  Washington to AH, 10 July 1787, *PAH* 4:225.

15  *PAH* 4:234.

16  *PAH* 4:235, 238, 243.

17  *PAH* 4:253.

## CHAPTER 7: POWER OF THE PEN

1   Frontispiece to Max M. Edling, *A Revolution in Favor of Government: Origins of the U.S. Constitution and the Making of the American State* (New York: Oxford University Press, 2003). Emphases in the original.

2   *The Daily Advertiser* (New York), 21 July 1787, in *PAH* 4:229–232.

3   *New York Journal*, September 20, 1787, in Chernow, *Alexander Hamilton*, 245, and *PAH* 4:281.

4   George Washington to AH, 18 October 1787, *PAH* 4:284.

5   Katherine Schuyler Baxter, *A Godchild of Washington* (London and New York, F. Tennyson Neely, 1897), 219.

6   Archibald McLean to Robert Troup, 11 October 1788, in Allan McLane Hamilton, *The Intimate Life of Alexander Hamilton* (New York: Charles Scribner's Sons, 1910), 82. Letter reprinted online at http://floridaverve.org/foundingnotesprinting-the-federalist-paper/

7   AH "Remarks on the Provisional Peace Treaty in the Continental Congress," *PAH* 3:295.

8   William Pierce, "Character Sketches of Delegates to the Constitutional Convention," in Farrand, *Records of the Federal Convention*, 3:89.

9   James Madison to George Washington, 16 April 1787, *The Papers of James Madison*, eds. Robert A. Rutland and William M. E. Rachal (Chicago: The University of Chicago Press, 1975), 9:383–85.

10  Robert Hendrickson, *The Rise and Fall of Alexander Hamilton* (New York: Van Nostrand Reinhold, 1985), 102.

11  When we cite any essay from *The Federalist* by number, we offer no further reference. There are countless print editions and ways to access *The Federalist* in print or on the Internet.

12  Quotations are from Hamilton's speech to the Constitutional Convention on June 18 and from the *Federalist* No. 69.

13  *Documentary History of the Ratification of the Constitution (DHRC)*, eds. Merrill Jensen et al, (Madison: State Historical Society of Wisconsin, 1976—), appendices for volumes 13–18.

14  For reprintings of Wilson's speech, see *DHRC* 13:337–338 and 344.

15  For reprintings of the *Federalist* essays, see *DHRC* 19:540–49.

16  Archibald McLean to Robert Troup, 11 October, 1788, in Allan McLane Hamilton, *Intimate Life of Alexander Hamilton*, 82.

17  *Cohens v Virginia*, Legal Information Institute, Cornell University Law School: https://www.law.cornell.edu/supremecourt/text/19/264

18  Ray Raphael, *Constitutional Myths* (New York: The New Press, 2013), 124.

19  Pamela C. Corley, Robert M. Howard, and David C. Nixon, "The Supreme Court and Opinion Content: The Use of the *Federalist Papers*," *Political Research Quarterly* 58:2 (June 2005): 336.

20  For the full story of the title's transformation, see Raphael, *Constitutional Myths*, 106–110.

## CHAPTER 8: POWER OF THE PURSE

1   AH to James Duane, 3 September 1780, *PAH* 2:404.

2   *Journal of the House of Representatives*, 21 September, 1789, 1:117. Library of Congress, American Memory, A Century of Lawmaking. http://memory.loc.gov/cgi-bin/query/r?ammem/hlaw:@field(DOCID+@lit(hj001165)

3   AH, "Report on the Public Credit," 9 January 1790, *PAH*, 6:65–168.

4   *PAH*, 6:99–103.

5   *Journal of William Maclay*, 29 January, 1790, and 9 February, 1790, 189 and 194. Library of Congress, American Memory, A Century of Lawmaking. http://memory.loc.gov/cgi-bin/query/r?ammem/hlaw:@field(DOCID+@lit(mj0014)

6   George Washington to AH, 16 February 1791, *PAH* 8:50.

7   AH to Washington, 21 February 1791, *PAH* 8:57–58.

8   Washington to AH, 23 February 1791, *PAH* 8:134–135.

9   AH to Washington, 23 February 1791, *PAH* 8:135.

10  Hamilton to —, 21 September 1791, *PAH* 12:408.

11  Philip Schuyler to AH, 29 January 1792, *PAH* 10:580–581.

12  AH to —, 21 and 26 September 1791, *PAH* 12:408

and 480. See also letters to Charles Cotesworth Pinckney, 10 October 1792, and John Steele, 15 October 1792, *PAH* 12:544 and 567–69.

13 *Journal of William Maclay*, 24 May, 1790, 272.

14 Thomas Jefferson to William Short, 3 January 1793, *The Papers of Thomas Jefferson*, ed. John Catanzariti (Princeton, NJ: Princeton University Press, 1992), 25:14–17.

15 AH and Henry Knox to Washington, 2 May 1793, *PAH* 14:386.

16 Morton J. Frisch, ed., *The Pacificus-Helvidius Debates* (Indianapolis, IN: Liberty Fund, 2007), 1.

17 AH, "Pacificus Number 1," in Frisch, *Pacificus-Helvidius Debates*, 12–13. Emphases added.

18 Jefferson to James Madison, 7 July 1793, *The Papers of James Madison*, 15:43, or Frisch, *Pacificus-Helvidius Debates*, 54.

19 *The Federalist* No. 75. Emphases added.

20 Jefferson to Madison, 8 September 1793, *PAH* 15:325n1.

21 Angelica Schuyler Church to Jefferson, 27 November 1793, *The Papers of Thomas Jefferson*, 27:449–450.

22 Jefferson to Edmund Randolph, 3 February 1794, *The Papers of Thomas Jefferson*, 28:15–16.

23 AH to Edward Carrington, 26 May 1792, *PAH* 11:440–441.

24 AH to Washington, 11 November 1794, *PAH* 17:366.

25 Chernow, *Alexander Hamilton*, 474.

26 Washington to AH, 29 May 1794, *PAH* 16:441–42.

27 AH to William Hamilton, 2 May 1797, *PAH* 21:77–78.

## CHAPTER 9: POLITICS AND SCANDAL

1 *The Argus, or Greenleaf's New Daily Advertiser*, July 20, 1795, *PAH* 18:486n33.

2 Seth Johnson to Andrew Craigie, 25 July 1795, *PAH* 18:485n33.

3 George Cabot to Rufus King, 27 July 1795, in Henry Cabot Lodge, *Life and Letters of George Cabot* (Boston: Little, Brown, 1878), 82–83. The incident is discussed in Joanne B. Freeman, *Affairs of Honor: National Politics in the New Republic* (New Haven: Yale University Press, 2001), xiii–xiv and 295n1.

4 *The Argus*, 20 July 1795, *PAH* 18:486.

5 For the back-and-forth arrangements of the duel between Hamilton and Nicholson, and Nicholson's eventual apology, see *PAH* 18:471–474, 489–491, 501–503.

6 Edward Livingston to Margaret Beekman Livingston, 20 July 1795, *PAH* 20:42n2.

7 George Washington to AH, 14 July 1795, *PAH* 18:466–67.

8 For Hamilton's authorship of Washington's Farewell Address, see *PAH* 20:168–183, 264–288, and 294–303.

9 Fisher Ames to Oliver Wolcott, 26 September 1796, *Memoirs of the Federal Administrations of George Washington and John Adams*, ed. George Gibbs (New York: n.p., 1846), 384.

10 AH to James Wilson, 25 January 1789, *PAH* 5:248.

11 Robert Troupe to Rufus King, 16 November 1796, in James Roger Sharp, *American Politics in the Early Republic* (New Haven, CT: Yale University Press, 1993), 149; AH to King, 4 May 1796, *PAH* 20:158.

12 Abigail Adams to John Adams, 31 December 1796, *The Adams Papers: Adams Family Correspondence* (Cambridge, MA: Harvard University Press, 2013), 11:472–75.

13 John Adams to Abigail Adams, 9 January 1797, 11:486–87.

14 AH to *The Daily Advertiser*, 15 September 1787, *PAH* 4:252.

15 *PAH* 21:250–51.

16 AH to Elizabeth Hamilton, 4 September 1791, *PAH* 9:172–73.

17 Maria Reynolds to AH, 23 January to 18 March 1792, *PAH* 10:557.

18 *PAH* 21:238–267.

19 James Callender to Thomas Jefferson, 28 September 1797, *The Papers of Thomas Jefferson* 29:536-537.

20 Washington to AH, 21 August 1797, *PAH* 21:214.

21 "The Stand No. 1," *PAH* 21:384-85.

22 AH to General Lafayette, 6 October 1789, *PAH* 5:425.

23 AH to Lafayette, 6 January 1799, *PAH* 22:404.

24 Mistakenly, this force is often called the "Provisional Army," which was authorized seven weeks earlier, on May 28, 1798, but was never raised. See *PAH* 22:4, 385, 387.

25 Washington to AH, 14 July 11798, *PAH* 22:18.

26 Washington to John Adams, 25 September 1798, *The Papers of George Washington*, Retirement Series, eds. W. W. Abbot and Edward G. Lengel (Charlottesville: University Press of Virginia, 1999), 3:36–44.

27 Philip Schuyler to AH, 31 January 1799, *PAH* 22:450.

28 AH to James Gunn, 22 December 1798, *PAH* 22:388–90.

29 AH to Harrison Gray Otis, 16 January 1799, *PAH* 22:440–41.

30 AH to Francisco de Miranda and AH to King, 22 August 1798, *PAH* 22:154–56.

31 AH to Pickering, 9 and 21 February 1799, *PAH* 22:475, 492–93.

32 Lear's transcript is reprinted in Peter R. Henriques, *The Death of George Washington: He Died as He Lived* (Mt. Vernon, VA: The Mount Vernon Ladies' Association, 2000), 7075.

**CHAPTER 10: HONOR**

1 Nancy Isenberg, *Fallen Founder: The Life of Aaron Burr* (New York: Penguin, 2008), 199.

2 John Sedgwick, *War of Two: Alexander Hamilton, Aaron Burr, and the Duel That Stunned the Nation* (New York: New American Library, 2016), 289.

3 Edward Larson, *A Magnificent Catastrophe: The Tumultuous Election of 1800* (New York: Free Press, 2007), 103.

4 AH to John Jay, May 7, in *PAH* 24:465.

5 Editorial note, ibid.

6 "A Letter from Alexander Hamilton, concerning the public Conduct and Character of John Adams, Esq., President of the United States," *PAH* 25:169–234.

7 AH to Oliver Wolcott Jr., 16 December 1800; AH to Theodore Sedgwick, 20 December 1800; and Sedgwick to AH, 10 January 1801, *PAH* 25:257, 270, 311.

8 Joanne B. Freeman, *Affairs of Honor: National Politics in the New Republic* (New Haven, CT: Yale University Press, 2002), xv.

9 For a list of Hamilton's narrowly averted duels, see Freeman, *Affairs of Honor*, 326–327.

10 Editorial notes, *PAH* 25:435–437.

11 AH to Richard Kidder Meade, 27 August 1782, *PAH* 3:150–151.

12 AH to Philip A. Hamilton, 5 December 1791, *PAH* 9:560–561.

13 AH to Elizabeth Hamilton, 20 March 20, 1793, *PAH* 26:95–96.

14 In Chernow, *Alexander Hamilton*, 665.

15 AH to William Cooper, 6 September 1802, *PAH* 26:52–53.

16 Joseph Ellis, *Founding Brothers: The Revolutionary Generation* (New York: Alfred A. Knopf, 2001), 32–36. The full interchange of letters between Burr, Hamilton, and their respective seconds is in *PAH* 26:235–312.

17 AH to Elizabeth Hamilton, 4 July 1804, *PAH* 26:293.

18 AH to Elizabeth Hamilton, 19 July 1804, *PAH* 26:308.

19 David Hosack to William Coleman, 17 August 1804, *PAH* 26:344.

20 Oliver Wolcott Jr., to his wife, 11 July 1804, *PAH* 26:317.

**EPILOGUE**
1 James McHenry to AH, 3 January 1791, *PAH* 7:409-410.

2 William Kent, *Memoirs and Letters of James Kent* (Boston: Little, Brown and Co., 1898), 281–282.

3 Allan McLane Hamilton, *The Intimate Life of Alexander Hamilton*, 111.

4 Charles R. King, ed., *The Life and Correspondence of Rufus King* (1900), 6:618–619; *PAH* 20:172–173.

5 Darren Staloff, *Hamilton, Adams, Jefferson: The Politics of Enlightenment and the American Founding* (New York: Hill and Wang, 2005), 49, 126.

6 Stephen F. Knott, *Alexander Hamilton and the Persistence of Myth* (Lawrence, KS: University of Kansas Press, 2002), 64, 119.

7 William Ander Smith, "Henry Adams, Alexander Hamilton, and the American People as a 'Great Beast,'" *The New England Quarterly* 48:2 (June, 1975), 219–220.

8 Knott, *Alexander Hamilton and the Persistence of Myth*, 134, 163, 175; Julian Boyd, ed., *The Papers of Thomas Jefferson* (Princeton: Princeton University Press, 1971), 18:611–688.

9 Knott, *Hamilton and the Persistence of Myth*, 152.

10 Ibid., 157–158.

11 Gordon Wood, "The Greatest Generation," *New York Review of Books*, March 29, 2001.

12 David McCullough, "The Argonauts of 1776," *New York Times*, July 4, 2002.

13 Joseph Ellis, *Founding Brothers*, 17.

14 Chernow, *Alexander Hamilton*, 6.

# Image Credits

Alamy: © Everett Collection, Inc.: 134; © Andrew Woodley: 3

Architect of the Capitol: 156, back cover

Art Resource: New York Public Library: 177, 245; © The Art Archive/Museum of the City of New York: 90

Bridgeman Images: 18, 32, 46, 70; © Museum of the City of New York: 77; © Museum of Fine Arts Boston: 49; © New York Historical Society: 259; © Ken Walsh/Private Collection: 250

Chris Bain: 34, 74, 75 bottom, 82, 107

Courtesy of Brown University: John Carter Brown Library: 9, 10, 11, 66

Courtesy of Christiansted National Historic Site: 13

Courtesy of Columbia University: University Archives, Rare Book and Manuscript Library: 25; Art Properties, Avery Architectural & Fine Arts Library: 117

Getty Images: ©MPI: 88; New York Historical Society: 254

© Granger Images: 36, 50, 96, 201, 214, 231

Courtesy of Heritage Auctions: 56

Internet Archive: 22, 29, 229, 247

iStock: © Xacto: cover (engraved patterns)

Library of Congress: ii, ix, 6, 15, 17, 35 top, 44, 59, 81, 87, 105, 124, 131, 153, 172, 180, 187, 190, 206, 219, 233, 234, 235, 236, 237, 238, 260, 268

Los Angeles County Museum of Art: 73

Courtesy of M/S Maritime Museum of Denmark: 12

Courtesy of Metropolitan Museum of Art: 48, 76, 140

National Archives: 83, 111, 224, 244

National Gallery of Art: cover (Hamilton), 143, 160, 165

New York Public Library: x, 20, 60, 65, 69, 75 top, 85, 86, 94, 95, 102, 116, 120, 123, 127, 133, 148, 150, 170, 192, 193, 205, 209, 215, 241, 242, 246 right, 248, 251, 255

Courtesy of National Guard: 42, 194

Private Collection: i, 63, 64, 106, 112, 184, 232, 252

Phil Scalia: 262

Shutterstock: © Julio Cortez/AP Photo: 35; © Olga Rutko: cover (rosettes)

Smithsonian Institution: 256; National Numismatic Collection: 179

Courtesy of Sotheby's: 175

Superstock: 78

Courtesy of the Walters Art Museum: iii, spine

Courtesy of West Point Museum, United States Military Academy: 55, 99

Courtesy of Wikimedia Foundation: 58, 108, 110, 114, 139, 159, 179 top; Brown: 68; Bureau of Engraving and Printing: 220, 232; Frick Collection: 7 2; Geographicus: 40, 43, 147; Gibbs Museum of Art: 227; NARA: 39, 137; National Portrait Gallery: 84; New York Public Library: 138; Princeton Art Museum: 53; Smithsonian Institution: 246 left258; White House: 188, 223, 235

Courtesy of Yale University: Beinecke Rare Book and Manuscript Library: 210; Yale University Art Gallery: 31, 51, 80, 118, 198

# About the Authors

MARIE RAPHAEL is the author of two historical novels, *Streets of Gold* (Persea, 2001) and *A Boy From Ireland* (Persea, 2007). For decades she has worked closely with her husband, Ray Raphael, frequently acting as research assistant and editor. Together they have co-authored two books, *The Complete Idiot's Guide to the Founding Fathers* and *The Spirit of '74: How the American Revolution Began*. Marie has taught literature and writing at Boston University, College of the Redwoods, and Humboldt State University. Marie and Ray live in Northern California.

RAY RAPHAEL's twenty books include *A People's History of the American Revolution* (The New Press, 2001; Harper Perennial, 2002; and The New Press, 2016); *The First American Revolution: Before Lexington and Concord* (The New Press, 2002); *Founding Myths: Stories that Hide Our Patriotic Past* (The New Press, 2004 and 2014); *Founders: The People Who Brought You a Nation* (The New Press, 2009); *Mr. President: How and Why the Founders Created a Chief Executive* (Alfred A. Knopf, 2012); *Constitutional Myths: What We Get Wrong and What We Get Right* (The New Press, 2013). With Alfred F. Young and Gary B. Nash he edited *Revolutionary Founders: Rebels, Radical and Reformers in the Making of the Nation* (Alfred A. Knopf, 2011). His most recent work is *The U. S. Constitution: The Citizen's Annotated Edition* (Vintage, 2016).

In 2013 Raphael received the Bay State Legacy Award from the Massachusetts Humanities Council for his contributions in public history. He has held research fellowships from the National Endowment for the Humanities and the Gilder Lehrman Institute of American History. He is an elected member of the American Antiquarian Society and an associate editor for the *Journal of the American Revolution*. His comprehensive, document-based lesson plans on the Constitution are available online at the Constitutional Sources Project (ConSource) website: http://www.consource.org/lessons/.

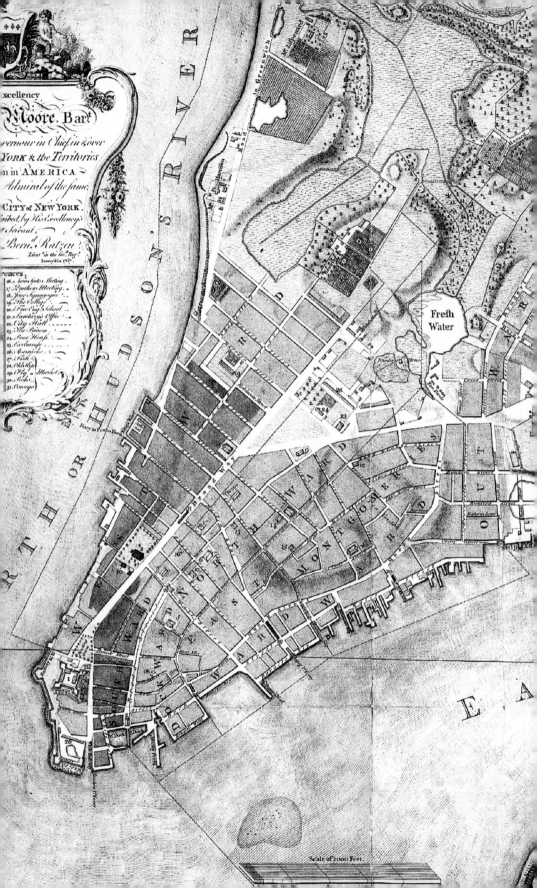